MW00478657

Politics & People

A WAYNESBORO STORY

Politics & People

A WAYNESBORO STORY

Frank S. Lucente

MARINER
PUBLISHING
BUENA VISTA, VA

Copyright © 2018 by Frank S. Lucente

All rights reserved, including the right of reproduction in whole or in part in any form without the express written permission of the publisher.

1   3   5   7   9   10   8   6   4   2

Library of Congress Control Number: 2018957234

Politics and People: A Waynesboro Story
Frank S. Lucente

p. cm.
1. Political Science: American Government—Local
2. Political Science: Commentary & Opinion
3. Political Science: Political Process—General

I. Lucente, Frank S., 1945– II. Title.
ISBN 13: 978-0-9992885-6-6 (softcover : alk. paper)

Mariner Publishing
An imprint of
Mariner Media, Inc.
131 West 21st Street
Buena Vista, VA 24416
Tel: 540-264-0021
www.marinermedia.com

Printed in the United States of America

This book is printed on acid-free paper meeting the requirements of the American Standard for Permanence of Paper for Printed Library Materials.

Dedication

To my son Sam,
whose short life inspires me to
live my life with purpose.

And to my six grandchildren—
Sophia, Julia, Mia, Lila Jane, Santino, and Vivian—
with the hope that someday
they will read this and
know my determination to
ensure a healthy future for them.

Table of Contents

ACKNOWLEDGMENTS
XI

INTRODUCTION
XIII

CHAPTER 1:
COMING TO WAYNESBORO
1

CHAPTER 2:
THE APPOINTMENT
13

CHAPTER 3:
FIRST YEAR ON COUNCIL
25

CHAPTER 4:
THE ELECTION OF 2006
45

CHAPTER 5:

THE MINORITY YEARS
55

CHAPTER 6:

THE WAYNE THEATRE
63

CHAPTER 7:

THE ELECTION OF 2008
77

CHAPTER 8:

A MATTER OF CODE
87

CHAPTER 9:

SAVING AND SPENDING
97

CHAPTER 10:

THE ELECTION OF 2010
111

CHAPTER 11:

THE MAYOR
119

CHAPTER 12:

THE TRIP TO CHINA
139

CHAPTER 13:

THE SCHOOL BOARD
151

CHAPTER 14:

CHICOPEE AND OPPORTUNITY PARK
161

CHAPTER 15:

THE ELECTION OF 2012
173

CHAPTER 16:

MY DANGEROUS DOG
199

CHAPTER 17:

THE TRASH ISSUE
211

CHAPTER 18:

STORMWATER
225

CHAPTER 19:

THE BUDGET PROCESS
235

CHAPTER 20:

WORKING TOGETHER
247

CHAPTER 21:

MOVING ON
261

Acknowledgments

Writing this book did not come naturally to me. It required a lot of research and revisiting, as I learned that memories are not to be trusted, especially mine.

The book would not have come about were it not for Janet Harvey, a dear friend who badgered me into writing about my experience as a Councilman. Janet coaxed me into Jo Ann Sabas's class on memoir writing. With Jo Ann's encouragement, I began this project.

Then an acquaintance led me to Kitty Sachs, who worked with me to turn my writings and recollections into a book. She is a former small town newspaper and magazine publisher, and her experience and skills were a good fit for the story I was trying to tell. Through our collaboration, I found the strength and reassurance to keep going.

Julia Bortle, the Clerk of the Council, helped me immensely by gathering the historical information essential to turning memories into factual accounts.

Last, but not least, is my wife, Betty. She read and re-read the work in progress and gave her unfiltered opinions and insights into how the book would be received. She put up with my ups and downs, mostly downs with this project, and for that I will be forever grateful.

Introduction

ike most five-year-old boys in Fairmont, West Virginia, my dream was to become a fireman–until I set a field ablaze. My friend Richard and I were playing with matches, starting little fires and stomping them out. One of us touched off a clump of dry weeds and the flames got ahead of us. We ran away.

Once the firemen had extinguished the fire, we snuck back to the scene of our crime. Nearby school kids had been drawn to the excitement during their lunch hour. They got a lift back to class on the firetruck. I was too young to be in school, but hopped aboard anyhow and walked the three blocks home. We lucked out. No property damage resulted from our foolishness, and I've never told anyone.

Next, I pictured myself as a jet pilot, until a nauseating Ferris wheel ride proved I wasn't made of the right stuff. My screaming started as soon as the wheel began its descent and didn't stop until the operator unloaded me mid-ride.

And finally, I set my sights on a job for which I was better suited. I wanted to be the president of the

Me around five years old
at home in Watson, West Virginia.

United States. At the age of 17, now on a career path, I was motivated to live my young life on the straight and narrow. I joined the US Naval Reserve to make respectable use of the summer between my junior and senior year of high school.

The regular Navy's eight-week basic training at the Great Lakes Naval Training Center sounded like a good choice. I sacrificed a promising summer with a beautiful girlfriend, thinking the training would put me on the road to manhood. The "Dear John" letter broke my heart.

Around the seventh week in training, I was diagnosed with walking pneumonia and admitted to the naval hospital. It took me three months to recover. I returned home in late November 1962, well into my senior year. My principal had me wait for the second semester before re-entering, and I would have to make up the first semester in summer school. Thankfully, I was allowed to wear a cap and gown and walk across the stage with my classmates at graduation. The principal handed me a mock diploma. The real one came when I finished summer school.

By the time I completed my basic training, I'd had my fill of the Navy. I asked at the Reserve Center if there was some way that I could put off the inevitable. A college deferment was the answer.

I entered Fairmont State College in my hometown and became a good-enough student. One year in, President Kennedy was assassinated, and Vice President Johnson moved into the White House. He began sending more troops to Vietnam and deferments were being curtailed. I was desperate for a way to stay out of the Navy.

I applied for Reserve Officer Candidate school (ROC), designed to train you as an officer while you're attending college. I was required to attend two eight-week training sessions in Newport, Rhode Island. I did the first session the summer between my sophomore and junior year.

After I graduated from Fairmont with a Bachelor of Arts degree in psychology, I returned to Rhode Island for my second eight-week training session. That completed, I was awarded a commission of Ensign in the US Navy, and there was no way out of active duty. All told, I had six months of basic training under my belt. I had built up my confidence and proudly considered myself to be an officer and a gentleman. I was ready to take on my ambitious plan to become the president of the United States.

My "dream sheet" as the Navy called it, asked what I would like to do as a naval officer. I wrote, "Just please don't assign me to the communication school," which was located right across the street from the ROC school I had just attended. I had no interest in the field of communications, and if I was sent there, I would have to report for duty on Monday right after receiving my commission on Saturday. I was hoping for a little leave time.

And please don't assign me to an aircraft carrier. I had heard that an aircraft carrier is a dead end for a naval officer's career because they are awash in ensigns and junior-grade lieutenants. Assign me to a naval destroyer where there are only four or five officers who each have critical roles and a chance to really show their stuff.

Wouldn't you know, they assigned me to communications school and then to the USS *Randolph*, an aircraft carrier—a slap in the face. I failed communications school because my heart wasn't in it. When I reported to the *Randolph*, I told them that I had failed communications school, certain that they would re-assign me. Instead, they recommended correspondence courses, and I spent the remainder of my enlistment in communications.

Once I returned to civilian life, I entered graduate school at Marshall University in Huntington, West Virginia, earning a Master of Arts degree in Guidance & Counseling and a Master of Arts degree in Business Administration with a marketing specialty that fully prepared me for my life's work in sales.

The ideals and discipline taught to me during basic military training have been invaluable. I believe that all young adults should serve in the military for two years. If not the military, then the Peace Corps or some other program dedicated to serving others. There are life-long benefits to being a part of something bigger than one's self.

I swapped my ambition to become the president of the United States for an ambition to earn a Ph.D. and a million dollars by the age of 35. I never earned the Ph.D., but eventually I reached my financial goal and circled back around to an interest in holding elected office, just not the presidency.

In 1980, at the age of 35, I launched my political career by jumping into a House of Delegates race in West Virginia on the Republican ticket. This memoir of my letdowns and triumphs chronicles the processes of small town governments and the people who make them tick. I hope to encourage others to take up the torch.

CHAPTER 1

Coming to Waynesboro

When my grandfather got home from working in the mines, he was covered in black coal dust except for the whites of his eyes. He would disappear into the basement for a shower and re-appear a new man, ready to work in his vegetable garden. Like the gardens pictured in *Southern Living,* not a weed or blade of grass stood a chance.

Sometimes, he and I sat under his grape arbor and talked. I was captivated by him blowing parodi smoke through the stem of a dandelion. At around the age of five or six, I asked him what happens when a person dies. He answered quickly and certainly, "When you die, nothing, black, the end."

As I was growing up, I tried practicing Christianity for a while because I wanted to believe in an afterlife. But my grandfather's words are so firmly rooted in me that I keep coming back to "the end." His answer, so confidently given, is my motivation for making the best use of this lifetime.

When I first considered running for state office, my friends all but laughed at me and called me crazy. This little bit of light-hearted negativity was almost enough to make me stop before I started. I learned that if you don't have a strong constitution, your behavior will most likely be dictated by influences outside of yourself. I mustered the willpower to run for office in spite of them, and when they realized I wasn't to be swayed by their antics, they declared their support.

To run for a seat in the West Virginia House of Delegates, you must first win your chosen party's primary. As a social liberal and a fiscal conservative, my politics are not aligned precisely with one major party platform or the other. I didn't think that I could win the Democratic primary in 1980 because all the other Democratic candidates were incumbents, and incumbents are hard to beat. There were no incumbents running in the Republican primary, so I decided to run as a Republican.

Six delegates were to be elected to the House from my district. I came in fourth in the Republican primary, so it looked like I had a shot at one of the six seats in the general election, but instead, I finished eighth. Not surprisingly, the incumbent Democrats won every seat.

I felt good about the way I had run the race though. I had worked hard, used my head, studied all the books that I could find on how to run campaigns and win elections. I remember reading someplace that an election will be won or lost on a single event or situation that will work for or against a candidate, and over which the candidate has no control. In this case, the single situation was an immense, unmatchable outlay of cash. Jay Rockefeller (great-grandson of oil tycoon John D. Rockefeller) won the governor race and carried all the Democratic candidates for the House on his coattails. He spent about $30 for each of the 401,863 votes that he received, paying everyone and his brother to haul voters to the polls. One Democratic candidate won her campaign by merely handing out some balloons.

The local paper ran reports of the election spending under the headline "Lucente Spends Thousands." Rockefeller had spent approximately $12 million. That was the most that had ever been spent on a gubernatorial race up until that time.

If there had been an opening for me to run in the Democratic primary, I would have been one of those elected to the House on Rockefeller's coattails, but that was not in the cards. The awareness that nothing I could have done would have changed the outcome brought me some solace and fired me up for another race.

In 1982, I threw my hat back into the ring as a Republican to run against an undefeated long-term Democratic state Senator. I didn't win, but I made a respectable showing. This time, I blamed it on straight-ticket voting.

Rather than casting a vote for one candidate at a time, *straight-ticket voting* allows a voter to choose a party's entire slate of candidates for each partisan office with just a single ballot mark or punch. The candidates' names would appear in a column beneath the party's icon, a donkey for Democrats and an elephant for Republicans. Ballots were commonly designed that way around the 1960s and 70s. Straight ticket ballots can dramatically affect the outcome of an election. There are still nine states that allow it, but straight ticket voting was abolished in West Virginia in 2015.

Not discouraged, I ran again in 1984 as a Republican for the House of Delegates. I won in the primary, but I soon realized that the party was encouraging me to be out campaigning and spending my money to the party's benefit, but not supporting me personally as a candidate. A party member dropped by my home for a visit. He brought his own scotch, which he didn't offer to share, and behind my back, he told my wife that he thought I was dumber than Jay Rockefeller. Well, in my opinion, Jay was not very bright.

That kind of disloyalty and disrespect caused me to lose heart and resign from my nomination. The rude visitor was appointed to take my place on the ticket and he lost. Asking people to vote for me had left a bad taste in my mouth. After

> **I would never run again unless I was asked to do so.**

I resigned, I adopted a new political credo, which I've stuck with to this day: The voters ought to seek the candidates, rather than the candidates seeking the voters. So I gave up pursuing office and decided that I would never run again unless I was asked to do so by the people. That took twenty years.

In 1983, I opened a small hot dog stand, which was the prototype for one of the businesses I run today. I named the stand for my father, Sam. My idea was to perfect the business to the point where I could duplicate it and sell franchises for others to own and operate. I expanded Sam's Hot

Dogs Inc. into five stands over the next seven years.

In the spring of 1990, our family moved to Waynesboro, Virginia, where my wife had taken a job as Chief Nursing Officer at Augusta Medical Center. I sold all five hot dog stands as franchises. With a new direction, Sam's flourished and grew as my family embraced the Waynesboro community and its charitable organizations.

In 1998, as a big brother in the Big Brother, Big Sister organization, I met with Waynesboro's youth probation officer, Frank Dooms, on a discipline matter concerning my "little brother" who had gotten into a bit of trouble. Dooms told me that the community didn't offer healthy organized activities for the kids. A lot of them have no support system or encouragement and consequently suffer from low self-esteem.

I had some self-esteem issues as a kid and knew what that felt like. On long summer days, my buddies and I chose sides and played baseball on a field known as the sandbank until dark. In the spring of 1957, when I was 12, the tryouts for little league were being held at the junior high baseball field on 5th Street in Fairmont, West Virginia. A few of us decided to see if we could make the team.

Over several days, Coach Dick Hup and Assistant Coach Charlie Himes sized us up. I felt I wasn't very good, but 12 was the top of the age limit and gave me a bit of an advantage over the younger kids. I made the team, but my ten-year-old brother didn't. I'm still bothered when I picture him going up the street crying on the long walk home.

Winning was important to the coaches, so I almost never got to play. Robert Ferrise and I were stuck on the bench establishing a bond with each other. One day, I got to play left field, and a fly ball came my way. It was an easy catch, but the ball bounced out of my glove and fell to the ground, allowing a run or two to be scored. My fate was sealed.

I don't remember having a single chance at bat during the whole regular season, but I do remember my last act as a member of the team. It was a typical game. Some were under the lights, but this was a day game. Assistant Coach Himes was substituting for Coach Hup. Ferrise and I were warming the bench as usual. Our team was up 22–7, and in those days there was no slaughter rule. I was excited when the crowd started to chant, "Put in the subs!" But Himes refused, proclaiming he wanted a big win for Coach Hup. Ferrise and I stood up, looked at each other, and without saying a word marched out of the dugout and across the field. We exited between first and second base and impetuously threw our gloves into the West Fork River on our way home.

My younger brother who hadn't made the team spent his days playing ball with his friends back at the sand bank while I warmed the bench on the Little League field. I learned that winning isn't everything that summer, and I didn't get the confidence-building accolades received by kids who are good at sports. And my loving, well-meaning mother, in order to shelter me from disappointment, taught

CHRIS GRAHAM/Staff

Frank Lucente and Lloyd Holloway point out the new sign above the front entrance to the Boys and Girls Club of Waynesboro headquarters on East Main Street. The building was named to honor late civic leader Paul Freed.

The News Virginian, August 4, 1998

me that I was a commoner and shouldn't expect much from myself or life. Thank goodness for my dad, a coal miner like his father, who only finished third grade yet managed to keep a positive outlook. He believed in me and encouraged me to get an education, convincing me that I could do anything I set my mind to.

I felt these Waynesboro kids that Dooms was talking about needed strong role models who believed in them and experiences that would help them develop confidence and determination. I had seen the positive effect of the Boys & Girls Club of America organization as an adult back in West Virginia. They describe their program as an affordable, safe place to learn, play, and grow, providing supporting relationships with caring mentors, etc. It was clear to me that Waynesboro, with its population of 20,000 was in need of a Boys & Girls Club. I introduced Dooms to the idea, and he supported it enthusiastically.

I got in touch with the national organization and with their guidance laid the groundwork. I recruited other local citizens to form a steering committee. My role was that of a facilitator. My passion for giving these kids an opportunity was contagious, and I was quite successful at raising money, rounding up resources, and laying out plans. Who can say no to kids?

We gratefully accepted a contribution of $25,000 from Waynesboro City Council. While we had no intention of relying on government funding, we were pleased to hear the Council say they could help again the next year if need be.

One of my friends, Lloyd Holloway, a retired car dealer, donated his 40,000-square-foot Ford dealership building to the cause. Holloway and I, along with Leroy Wilkerson, owner of several local Burger King franchises, co-signed a loan for a $100,000 to renovate the building as home to the Boys & Girls Club.

In September 1999, the club opened. It was off to a good start for the first six months. Kids joined, programs were added, and costs grew. We decided to take Council up on its offer for more money. Surprisingly, it took some convincing to get them to make a second contribution.

Through this process, I discovered that in many ways City Council was heedless and ineffective when it came to addressing the needs of the Waynesboro community. One Councilman was literally sleeping during meetings. I started a drive to find a couple of promising candidates to run for office. Some friends and I began recruiting energetic people with fresh ideas to run against those who had served on Council too long.

But I had to put politics on the back burner when my 27-year-old son Sam, named after my father, was diagnosed with lymphoma of the stomach in December of 2001. Initially, we were told that his disease was 90 percent curable. He was presented with a couple of treatment options. Surgery didn't seem like the right way to go, and chemotherapy and radiation made only slight temporary advances. My wife and I made certain he had the best possible medical help locally as well as at Duke, but with each setback and failed experiment his chances of survival decreased. After an eight-month battle, Sam died on August 6, 2002. I loved him more than words can express, and I spent the next years of my life learning to live with my grief. To honor Sam's personal commitment to a healthy planet, I began recycling everything I could, and I redoubled my efforts to benefit the environment and society in the time I'm privileged to have. I gradually got back to my interest in waking up Waynesboro's City Council.

CHAPTER 2

The Appointment

There are five seats on the Waynesboro City Council: one seat for a resident of each of four wards (A, B, C, and D) and one at-large seat that can be filled by a resident of any of the four wards. An at-large candidate must declare him or herself to be an at-large candidate. More than one person can run for each ward seat as well as for the at-large seat. The person with the most votes per ward wins that ward's seat.

Council members are elected to four-year terms on a staggered basis. A registered city voter can vote for one candidate for each of the wards that is up for re-election, plus one at-large candidate when that seat is up for re-election. In the 2002 election, seats in wards D and C were up for re-election. In 2004, wards A and B and the at-large seat were up for re-election. That same cycle is repeated every four years.

In 2002, the Ward D incumbent was Dubose Egleston. He had been an okay Councilman for four years but, in my opinion, didn't make the best choices for the city. I got to know a group of political conservatives who acted as unofficial recruiters of qualified residents to run for local offices. They shared my opinion of Egleston, and we lined up Reo Hatfield to run against him.

Hatfield was a bigger than life civic-minded man with a generous spirit and a great big ego. He had previously served a term on Council from 1994–98 and was Vice Mayor the last two years of his term. He was captain of the reserve police force and later became its chief. He was the president of a successful transportation/distribution company and ran the business. He is credited with the idea of creating a truce to end the feud that began in 1865 between the Hatfields and McCoys. He and Bo McCoy of Kentucky drafted a treaty, which they ceremonially signed on June 14, 2003.

He defeated Egleston by just a few hundred votes.

Egleston has doggedly run again and again for office and presently serves in an elected position on the Headwaters Soil & Water Conservation District.

Lemuel Irvin, the Ward C incumbent, was challenged by Portia Bass as well as Nancy Dowdy, the candidate the conservative recruiters promoted. Dowdy was a life-long resident of Waynesboro. She was employed by Invista (formerly DuPont) as an Administrative Assistant for the Global Lycra Expansion team. She was elected by a wide margin. Irvin, who gave 16 years of honorable service to the city, died in 2008.

The general feeling in the community was that Council was much improved after the 2002 election cycle, so I felt that the recruiters' involvement in the process was well worth the time and energy we put in.

My association with City Council members, in combination with my commitment to the Boys & Girls Club, sent other civic involvements my way. I was asked by Council members to serve on the Waynesboro Redevelopment & Housing Authority Board of Directors. The board was made up of seven members, but Council felt there was too much attention being given to Section 8 (federal government's low-income designation) and low-income housing. They added two seats with the intention of improving communication between the board and Council and shifting the board's priorities. I was appointed by Council to fill one of the new seats.

Eddie DeLapp, the Director of the Board, was disturbed by the change, suspicious that Council had an ulterior motive. After being appointed, I asked if he would show me around and educate me as to the workings of the board. He showed me the properties owned and managed by the agency. During our ride, I explained that Council was concerned that the Housing Authority was burdening the city with more public housing than it could accommodate.

He explained that the new housing was privately owned and built by carpenters in training and paid for by the homeowners with financing made available through the Housing Authority. The housing stock was scattered throughout the city with no more than three in any one neighborhood. All the homes are owner-occupied.

I was very impressed. The Housing Authority owned apartment buildings throughout the city that they managed and rented to employed income-qualified applicants at low cost. The apartments were very well kept.

The Council's concern about Section 8 housing was unwarranted. They didn't understand that Section 8 is a program, not a place. The government-qualified participants are free to choose any housing that meets the requirements of the program and are not limited to units located in subsidized housing projects. The designation travels with the qualified participants wherever they move, and while not common, some participants can purchase a home rather than rent. It's a matter of a landlord or mortgage holder being willing to work within the program. So, our Housing Authority has no control over how many Section 8-qualified residents move in or out of Waynesboro. Once I understood the situation, I told him I thought the Council just needed more information. Our conversation quickly led to an improved relationship between the board and Council.

DeLapp was a very competent administrator, known throughout Virginia as one of the best housing directors. He was a master at writing proposals for state and federal grants that funded the building of low-cost housing, and he never asked the city for any money. In fact, the Housing Authority voluntarily paid Waynesboro a sum of money every year because they were exempt from property taxes.

I was able to help renegotiate some contracts and discount some obligations to the board's financial advantage. It was most gratifying to be in a position to give deserving residents a leg up when it comes to housing and it was a pleasure to work with DeLapp.

I dabbled in the 2004 City Council election, campaigning for the incumbents. Tim Williams ran unopposed in Ward A. Tom Reynolds defeated Howard Monroe (aka Brother Yhwh) in Ward B, and Chuck Ricketts defeated Dubois Egleston for the at-large seat. The headline in *The News Virginian* read "Ricketts Reynolds Breeze to Re-Election."

In 2005, Councilman Ricketts was appointed Judge of the Circuit Court, so he had to resign from City Council. I was excited when I heard about that seat opening up because I had become interested in serving on Council. I thought I might have a chance at being appointed to the vacant seat.

I got calls from Councilmen Williams and Hatfield. They encouraged me to apply for Ricketts's spot. Remember my credo? Waiting until asked to serve? The time had come. It was an at-large seat that a candidate from any of the four wards could fill.

Those interested in filling the seat were to submit applications. Once the applications were reviewed, the candidates would be interviewed by Council in a closed session. Then Council would vote to decide which one would fill the unexpired term.

I felt well qualified to fill this seat. Holding two master's degrees from Marshall University, I probably had the most education of any of the nine candidates who came forward, and I had some experience in the workings of the city. Also, Williams and Hatfield had asked me to run, so that was already two of the votes needed. They suggested I chat individually with the other two Council members, Dowdy and Mayor Reynolds. Turns out that wasn't a very good suggestion, and I wish I hadn't taken it. Even though there was nothing underhanded about it, my approach was resented, taken as kowtowing.

Todd Foster, the politically-oriented editor of *The News Virginian*, had a fit when he heard of the closed session interviews. He accused Council of malfeasance and insisted through his editorial pieces that there be a public forum to consider the candidates.

Council bowed to the newspaper's pressure and allowed them to conduct the questioning. In spite of the misstep with Dowdy and Reynolds, I felt confident going into the open forum. I thought that I came across as knowledgeable when I answered the questions. Probably my most rousing comment was that the city government was growing faster than the city. I emphasized that I was in favor of less government and more private enterprise.

(This is an ongoing concern. As I write this memoir in 2018, Council just passed a budget of $49.5 million with a seven-cent property tax increase.

Waynesboro has the same population with the same needs that it had in 2005 when the sufficient budget was $35 million. That's a 41 percent budget increase over 12 years.)

But I was in for a rude awakening. The next morning, the newspaper printed that I came across like a poker player holding aces, pompous and overly confident because of the favors owed me for helping other Council members get elected. I was baffled when they called me a good old boy because I had only lived in Waynesboro for 15 years. And also, I am a poker player and I know that a player holding aces doesn't let on that he's holding aces — bad analogy.

Council met behind closed doors on April 25, 2005, and I was unanimously appointed to fill the at-large seat. Members said complimentary things about my appointment to my face, but I found out later from Williams and Hatfield that there had been a big argument over candidates, ending up in a stalemate. If unable to come to an agreement, the City Code states that the Circuit Court Judge will make the decision. In that light, Dowdy reconsidered and cast her vote for me. Mayor Reynolds followed suit presenting a united front, and I was in. I resigned from the Housing Authority Board and was replaced there by Tom Reider.

THE NEWS VIRGINIAN

A Media General Newspaper

www.NewsVirginian.com

WAYNESBORO ■ STAUNTON ■ AUGUSTA COUNTY ■ NELSON COUNTY

50 cents

Lucente named to council

Members vote unanimously after an hour of deliberation

By BERTRAND M. GUTIERREZ
bgutierrez@newsvirginian.com

Political insider Frank Lucente was picked late Monday to fill the vacant Waynesboro City Council seat.

Council members took an hour behind closed doors to make up their minds. In the end, they unanimously chose a conservative applicant who said he supported low taxes and small government.

Lucente, however, also was a force behind the campaigns of council members Nancy Dowdy and Tim Williams, providing money to one and helping them get elected by collecting many of the necessary signatures to get them on the ballot.

A late call to Lucente was not immediately returned. The Waynesboro businessman is the franchiser of 40

Sam's Hot Dog Stands in four states, and he sits on the board of the city Redevelopment and Housing Authority.

Despite Lucente's contributions to the Williams campaign, Williams said he had no reason to recuse himself from the vote.

"I had many people circulating petitions for me," Williams said.

In announcing the decision, Mayor Tom Reynolds said there might have

LUCENTE

been "word on the street" that the process was a done deal from the beginning, but he said they simply picked the right man for the job.

"He rose to the top as we discussed each candidate," he said.

The selection process was

launched in a shroud of secrecy with the council members saying they would not release the names. Some of the candidates did not want their names to be known, the council members said initially.

The nine applicants' names were released, as the council tried to quell what they recognized were rumors of cronyism.

"I am greatly disappointed," candidate Stephen Winslow said. "People

See LUCENTE, Page A5

LUCENTE —

Continued from Page A1

kept telling me, 'Just understand, they're going to have to pick this guy.' It's very disappointing that all the critics of this process appear to be right."

The City Council was entrusted with the task of picking a replacement when former nine-year Councilman Chuck Ricketts resigned March 31 to accept a judgeship.

Councilman Reo Hatfield, meanwhile, stressed the fairness of the process.

"No decision had been made until tonight," he said.

Lucente is scheduled to be sworn in this week.

Contact Bertrand M. Gutierrez at 932-3561.

The News Virginian, April 26, 2005

The News Lead

Proud to serve our community for more than 100 yea

05 —————————| www.newsleader.com |—————————

Lucente appointed to fill vacant seat on council

Businessman will serve until 2008

By Jonathan D. Jones/staff
jjones@newsleader.com

WAYNESBORO — Frank Lucente is the man for the job.

At least that was the unanimous decision of City Council Monday night when it appointed Lucente to serve the remainder of Councilman Charles Ricketts' term.

"There were a lot of qualified people here," Mayor Thomas Reynolds said. "We really couldn't go wrong."

Council members cited his community involvement and business experience as reasons for selecting Lucente over eight other candidates.

Lucente, 60, is a businessman who was a founder of the Sam's Hot Dog chain that has 46 franchises. He also owns

Lucente

the downtown store. Lucente is a graduate of Fairmont State University and Marshall University. He has been active in the Boys & Girls Club in Waynesboro.

After acknowledging his candidacy two weeks ago, Lucente said he was asked by friends to apply for the seat.

Lucente had been rumored to be the choice long before council made

its announcement. Reynolds decried any assumptions that the decision had been made before council went into closed session Monday night to make its choice.

"I feel like we tried to involve the citizens of this community as much as possible," Reynolds said. All of the e-mails, letters and phone calls in support of individual candidates

Please see COUNCIL, back page this section

---

www.newsleader.com

Council

Continued from the front page

were taken into account, Reynolds said.

Councilman Reo Hatfield said it wasn't possible for the decision to have been made in advance because he had not talked to Reynolds or Vice Mayor Nancy Dowdy about their thoughts on a replacement until Monday night.

Reynolds said the board narrowed the list to five candidates by having an initial ballot. They then worked their way through the list of five until agreeing on Lucente. Reynolds said he was happy the council was able to make a unanimous choice.

"I think it's important for the council to move forward in unison," Reynolds said.

Lucente won't face election until Spring of 2008. Because of the city's charter, the appointment is for the remainder of the term.

Ricketts resigned last month in order to accept a judicial appointment.

The other eight candidates were: Gregory Bruno, Scott Coleman, Albert Cadaret II, DuBose Egleston Jr., Michelle Jenkins, Lorie Smith, Horace Studwell and Stephen Winslow.

"I'd like to thank the nine candidates," Dowdy said.

The News Leader, April 26, 2005

The newspaper had nothing good to say about my appointment to Council. They claimed that it was somehow pre-ordained, that the decision was a done deal before the vote. I don't guess they heard about the stalemate. I filled the seat vacated

The newspaper had nothing good to say.

by Ricketts with three years and two months remaining in the term. Williams and Hatfield and I were prudent like-minded people when it came to money, and we were now the majority vote on Council.

I had helped Councilwoman Dowdy get elected and considered her a friend. I was surprised to find that during the closed session, she had initially been opposed to my appointment. She and Mayor Reynolds kept their distance that first year.

I was highly motivated to be a valuable Councilman and accomplish beneficial things. I studied minutes from past meetings and learned all about the position to which I had been appointed. The City Charter says that the City Manager, the

Clerk of Council, the City Attorney, and the City Assessor work for City Council. For that reason, these positions are called charter appointments. More than 300 other city employees answer to the City Manager, so as a Councilman, I would be out of line to discuss city matters with an employee in Public Works, for example. Everything had to go through the City Manager.

It's a good system. If someone comes to City Council with a complaint, Council takes it to the City Manager. The manner in which Council has power within the system is in their role as the City Manager's boss.

I studied the rules and methods of governing a small city. I read the minutes from each of our Council meetings before they were approved to make sure they were correct. Owning my own business allowed me the flexibility of time to explore each issue facing Council. Having not been a highly motivated student in college, I surprised myself by quickly earning acceptance as the authority on the issues facing the City of Waynesboro.

CHAPTER 3

First Year on Council

Establishing the Boys & Girls Club is by far the best thing I have ever done. It prospers today with the help of private donors and public grants from local, state, and federal sources. It has become a valuable asset to our community, and I take a great deal of pride in the work I put into its development and accomplishments. Once appointed to Council, with the advantage of being in the majority, I was prepared to put the same kind of energy and commitment into getting crucial work done for the city.

The first thing on my agenda was to educate the public about the workings of City Council. It's really the job of a newspaper to keep an eye on the government and keep the residents informed, but sometimes *The News Virginian* didn't even bother to show up for Council meetings.

I thought of airing the meetings on closed-circuit TV. The meetings are public, and there's nothing to hide. I talked to Hatfield and Williams, and they agreed that it was a good idea. Dowdy and Reynolds thought it might lead to flamboyant speeches and showmanship in chambers. They shared the staff's concern that it could run into some money.

My son-in-law is a technology whiz who offered his expertise to set up the programming for free. There are those who are leery of anything for free but televising the Council meetings passed on a 3–2 vote. Some of the equipment was donated by the local hospital because they no longer needed it, and the city purchased a few items. It costs less than $5,000 a year to provide this service, which I believe is particularly beneficial to those who are homebound.

We achieved a lot over the next six months, but not without some in-fighting. It seemed Dowdy and Reynolds opposed most everything my like-minded colleagues and I tried to accomplish. As it turned out, one of their concerns about televising the meetings was not completely unfounded. We were seen battling over the issues on TV, and the community was greatly entertained by the drama. I fought determinedly for what I thought was best for the citizens. It was a while before I learned the value of compromise.

A quandary arose when the First Baptist Church in Waynesboro's Tree Streets Historic District requested an amendment to the overlay district ordinance. (Overlay districts provide a means to incorporate various development regulations across a specified area.) They wanted to tear down the house next door to the church in order to build a new building that better suited their needs. Other residents in the neighborhood didn't

"Not In My Back Yard!"

want the house torn down. They felt it could lead to more exceptions, more historic homes being replaced, loss of their historic district status and nature.

Regrettably, most people pay very little attention to the scope of what's going on in the community. But we've all heard of the NIMBY attitude. When it affects their own family or real estate, people fill Council chambers to say "Not In My Back Yard!" As a compassionate Councilman, you're torn. Residents on both sides of a conflict can have valid concerns, but they can't both win.

So, I made a suggestion to the City Planner. Rather than the Council making the decision, let's sit four or five residents from each side of the issue down together and have them work it out. I'm not certain exactly what compromise was reached, but the issue was soon resolved. The church never tore down the house, and the conversation resulted in the rewriting of the procedure for handling change in Waynesboro's historic districts.

Charlie Downs, while serving on the Waynesboro Disability Services Board, came to a Council meeting to ask for help getting a larger building for the Health Department. He complained that he'd made this request repeatedly to no avail. He asked Council to build a new building on a school property that was no longer in use.

We were heading into closed session, so I asked Downs to wait around to talk with me. (Closed sessions assure confidentiality about sensitive matters out of the public's eye. No official action can be taken during a closed session.) After the session, Downs and I discussed the Health Department's needs, and I promised to see what I could do. He was so pleased to just have someone listen to him.

A tour of the Health Department offices confirmed the needs. It was a tight space in an old tile building. The city was responsible for part of the cost of the current facility. The county and Staunton also paid a portion based on a percentage of use by their respective citizens. The state also contributed money, but an estimate to build and furnish a suitable new place was $3 million plus.

When it comes to money, I'm a consistent advocate of restraint. Waynesboro had relatively little debt when I came on Council. This was because previous Councils going back to the 60s had been of a conservative nature when it came to spending. The DuPont, Genicom, and Corban plants had brought well-educated professional engineers and administrators to the area. They got involved, served on City Council and the School Board, and other committees that boosted our community, and they handled the finances well. During the 70s, and up until recently, people seemed to be against debt in general. The thinking then was pay-as-you-go, and this carried into the way the city was run, maybe an aftermath of the Great Depression.

Waynesboro needed some infrastructure work including a new sewage treatment plant and a water treatment plant. We had at least 28 known stormwater management projects that needed to be tackled and our school buildings needed work. The cost to upgrade all of these systems was in the tens of millions. Previous Councils had put a lot of the maintenance off because of the huge expense. They kept everything patched together one way or another without spending much.

I believe it is wrong for any institution to pass debt along to future generations, and I respected the fact that the prior Councils didn't leave us with debt, but at some point, it all had to be properly addressed. I was determined to find affordable solutions for as much as I could, starting with the Health Department.

The old Crompton's Industrial Plant office building was up for rent. It was three stories tall with a nice entryway and big windows and spacious with plenty of restrooms and offices. I invited some people from the Health Department over to check it out. It was perfect! We could spend $10–15 thousand installing the necessary technology, and then share the rent with the other municipalities. The investment was quickly approved, and everyone congratulated us for saving the taxpayers millions.

The problems with the outdated sewage treatment system had been skirted for too long. Many stormwater lines were channeled into the sewage lines, which were broken and clogged by vegetation and roots. During heavy rains, we had to shut off the sewage lines to avoid overburdening the treatment plant. Once those lines were closed, the raw sewage would be circumvented into alternate pipes that had less capacity and emptied directly into South River. Because of the reduced capacity, those lines would often back up into the basements of the low-lying homes.

We rebuilt the sewage treatment plant to handle 450 percent its prior capacity. We replaced a lot of the sewage lines and re-routed stormwater lines so they no longer flowed into the sewage system. We met or exceeded all the Environmental Protection Agency (EPA) regulations for waste management for a city our size. The overall cost was $40 million.

The EPA required that we also build a new water treatment plant because of some flora content found in the samples of water taken from our water supply at Coyner Springs and our backup supply the Jefferson Well. The price for the new state-of-the-art system that filters out all impurities was $12 million.

The cost to greatly improve the city water and sewer facilities was covered in part by grants, but mostly by the fees paid by customers for the services on a per usage basis. None of the cost came out of the city's general fund, which is supplied by the collection of all kinds of city taxes.

Sometimes Dowdy and I worked well together, but more often, there were bitter feuds. She made very strong arguments. The suspicion that things in politics are decided in advance of the public's awareness is pretty much true. We often knew how issues would be resolved before we entered Council chambers. Every once in a while, a crowd would show up and turn an issue around, but like I said before, generally the citizens don't pay attention to what Council's doing.

We had some discretionary funds to donate to community non-profits. The budget was sort of locked in so that the same 10 or 12 organizations would get funded year after year. It wasn't a fair system, and it was quite rare for a new applicant to get a piece of the pie.

Habitat for Humanity had a house almost finished. The Director came to Council and requested a $6,000 donation to cover the cost of utility hook-up fees. She approached us as if this donation was a foregone conclusion, something we wouldn't hesitate to support. But given Council's donation budget, I thought $6,000 was too much to give to just one household. A gift that large should benefit multiple citizens. Dowdy was in agreement with me. She and I were both uncomfortable with the donation decision being in the hands of Council. Every decision you make turns someone against you, which puts a lot of pressure on elected officials. When Habitat's request was denied, they were very displeased.

We got out of the giving business, gratified to turn that over to the Community Action Partnership of Staunton, Augusta, and Waynesboro (CAPSAW). CAPSAW administers funds each year to non-profits and community action agencies based on merit. The funds are made available through various government block grant sources and the participating municipalities. Applications are submitted to a neutral Board of Directors, which includes one elected official from each of the three localities. I served on the board for a couple years and was pleased to participate in this evenhanded means of sharing the money.

The process of naming of the Thomas L. Gorsuch Municipal Building was challenging and fulfilling to me. Gorsuch was a modest, well-known, greatly-loved doctor and highly-valued member of the community. He did so much for Waynesboro and its people. He served as Mayor of the city, elder of his church, member of the Board of Directors of both Waynesboro Community Hospital and Augusta Health Care, and a member of many other boards and professional and civic organizations.

When he died, I wanted to do something significant to memorialize him. I suggested we name the courthouse building in his honor. Once word got out, I heard that some others in town were

Thomas L. Gorsuch Municipal Building

of the opinion that it should be named for a judge. I wrote up a two-page list of generous contributions Gorsuch had made to our community, pointing out that in many cases he never even charged his needy patients for his medical help.

Todd Foster at *The News Virginian* went with a suggestion of the Mayor's to have the public decide what to name the building. He ran a survey titled "Name That Building." According to his writing on July 8, 2005, Foster was disappointed with the initial responses:

> Come on people. If we had asked you to weigh in about our comics page, more than 100 of you would have responded by now....
>
> Only seven people so far have suggested namesakes for the city of Waynesboro's courthouse building at 250 S. Wayne Ave.
>
> Here are the vote totals so far:
>> Dr. Thomas L. Gorsuch. 3
>> Judge Humes J. Franklin. 1
>> J.B. Yount III. 1
>> Dr. Beverly Loesch. 1
>> Dr. Clarabelle Hopkins. 1
>
> These are all great candidates, but surely more than seven Waynesboro residents have an interest in this.

Call in your votes to us....

Meanwhile, here is some of the feedback we've gotten so far:

For Dr. Gorsuch: "He saved my life in 1979, continuing to be my physician until his retirement." One woman wrote, "Who else had the flags lowered upon his passing?"

One man wrote of Dr. Gorsuch, "Thanks for giving us the people an opportunity to express our respect and admiration for this gentleman...."

A women reader nominated current City Attorney J.B. Yount III who recently announced he would retire next spring. "Since J.B. spent so much time there with his services to the city, I think it's befitting. Thomas L. Gorsuch Building has a nice ring to it, but it's not the right kind of building for him."

Obviously, Foster had a name in mind, and two days later, he started his campaign. He wanted to name the building for William Sheppard.

...there's one name that has not been mentioned and should be. He's far and away the best choice for a building that stands for justice.

His name is William Sheppard.

Don't recognize the name? Why should you? There are no historical markers here or festivals honoring him or scholarships given out in his honor.

Yet he is the most famous Waynesboro native in history and was known worldwide for his crusade for human rights and justice in Africa and elsewhere.

He ran an extensive article about the Waynesboro native and his late 1800s humanitarian achievements. Wikipedia describes Sheppard as "one of the earliest African Americans to become a missionary for the Presbyterian Church. He spent 20 years in Africa…and is best known for his efforts to publicize the atrocities committed against the Kuba and other Congolese peoples by King Leopold II's Force Publique." As the survey continued, Gorsuch stayed in the lead and Foster continued to push for Sheppard, article after article.

The City Council could rename Waynesboro "Gorsuchville" and you'd get nary an argument from us. He touched hundreds, maybe thousands of lives here in profound ways that transcended medicine and healing.

Yet Sheppard's actions affected hundreds of thousands of people, maybe millions.

We're going to keep building a case for Sheppard, not out of political correctness, but because Sheppard's accomplishments were astonishing on a global scale, let alone when measured with a Waynesboro barometer.

Thirteen days in, the survey wrapped up and Sheppard came out ahead of Gorsuch 91 to 65. The headline read "Name that building vote is final—Sheppard wins."

But it wasn't up to the newspaper or its survey or the general public to decide on the name of the building. It was a decision for City Council to make. The following Sunday, Foster's editorial raised issues of racism and Waynesboro history. He said that readers had told him that there was no way that an all-white Council would name the building for a black man. He opined that if Waynesboro were a color-blind society the town would have already built monuments to Sheppard. I was fed up. I wanted to get this done. I brought it up at that Monday's City Council meeting even though it wasn't on the agenda, and we voted 3–2 in favor of naming the building for Gorsuch.

I was so pleased that we were able to honor Gorsuch in this way while his wife was still alive. Of course, my relationship with Foster at the paper went from bad to worse, but before the paper got involved, no one that I knew of could have even named the Sheppard guy.

The president of First Bank & Trust put in a request for a curb cut for access from the highway to a new bank building. Dowdy, Williams, and I had no problem with it, so it seemed like a done deal. Hatfield abstained because of a conflict of interest pertaining to partial ownership of a property across the street.

In general, Council unofficially agrees to avoid surprises, no one likes to be blindsided. But when First Bank's request came to a vote, Dowdy unexpectedly withdrew her support. She had given the rest of us no notice, and being caught off guard made us all look foolish. This caused a big rift between Dowdy and me. Of course, the bank president was livid. When it came time for her to run again for Council in 2006, I decided to

> **It seemed like a done deal.**

support her opponent, Pat Steele. And the rift grew wider.

Doug Walker was the City Manager in those days, and I visited with him before each Council meeting to catch up on issues. I was one of the few on Council who actually studied the budget. I was able to understand the financial statements because of my business background. I observed that the city's money was being managed in a misleading and inefficient way.

Waynesboro's budget includes two categories of expenditures. There's the general fund, and there are funds to support each of the city's three enterprises: garbage, water, and sewer. The flow of money was being intermingled. I realized, for example, that they were taking money out of the general fund to pay the garbage department's expenses for billing, collection, management, etc. So, it was difficult to tell whether or not the fees collected for garbage service actually covered the cost of the service. It was the same for water and sewage.

I suggested a new system to Walker that set up the garbage department to manage its own income and expenses independently and provide more accountability. He saw the merit and put the new system in place. Now it's much simpler to establish a fee for services based on the actual cost.

In December 2005, the Council was presented with an incentive plan by Collett & Associates and the Industrial Development Authority (IDA), now known as the Economic Development Authority (EDA). The plan was to develop a shopping center populated with well-known national retailers to be located on five acres in the northwest quadrant of the Outlet Village property.

Collett & Associates would invest a minimum of $25 million to develop the project and receive a tax rebate of $6.5 million from the city in installments over ten years. That was based on 80 percent of the real estate, meals, and sales taxes that would be paid over and above what was presently being collected from the property. The city's increase in tax revenue from the new center was conservatively projected to be $1,735,000 per year. Even with the substantial $6.5 million payout, Waynesboro would benefit. The city would still collect the other 20 percent of the taxes, approximately $350,000 in increased revenue each year until the rebate was paid off. Once the rebate was paid off, the city would collect the entire $1,735,000 in tax revenue each year. Collett & Associates would build the roads and install the street lights and other infrastructure required for the new center. There would be no other expense to the city.

This was a good deal in the minds of the Council members. It would draw more people to our city from rural Nelson County, Augusta County, and Stuarts Draft. We knew that the City of Staunton, as well as Augusta County, wanted this project, so we were highly motivated to do what it took to land it for Waynesboro.

The terms called for the tax rebate to be paid within ten years, and the city's staff thought we could pay it off in six. At the last minute, 3:00 p.m. on January 9, the day that the vote was to be taken at the regularly scheduled Council meeting, we were presented with a catch. The developer was asking for 6 percent interest on the unpaid balance after each year's rebate installment had been paid. For example, if we paid one million the first year, we would pay $330,000 (6 percent) interest on the balance of $5.5 million. This would cost the city more than a million dollars over the course of the deal. I was quite peeved by this last minute add-on, but I was the only one who wanted to fight it. I tried to convince Hatfield that the developer would not back out at this late date even if we resisted the additional demand. My suspicion was that they knew how hungry we were to get this done and figured they could at least give the interest thing a shot. If it didn't fly, they would not have lost anything. We could have counter bluffed and said no, and if they threatened to pull out, we could have backed off and agreed to pay the interest. But we will never know because I didn't have the support of Council to try it.

That evening in the presence of all the attorneys, realtors, and IDA members, Council passed a resolution on a 5–0 vote to accept the deal. The IDA members immediately retired to Room 106 of the municipal building to adopt their own policy resolution. The deal was done.

Three years later, the idea of having the EDA (formerly IDA) take out a loan to pay the developers off was introduced. The loan from the local bank would be repaid over a 10-year period at a reduced interest rate of 3.85 percent. So, on April 13, 2009, Council passed a resolution authorizing the EDA to borrow the funds. The new arrangement reduced the annual installment, as well as the overall amount of interest paid. That loan has now been paid off. The increase in tax revenue to the city paid by the

Town Center and its tenants is more than $1 million a year.

CHAPTER 4

The Election of 2006

Williams, Hatfield, and I worked well together as the majority on City Council. Brett Frank, Director of the Economic Development for the city, branded us "the Three Amigos," and it wasn't long before the newspaper and some of the townspeople followed suit. Nevertheless, I strived to be an effective Councilman and use the office to make positive advances for the community. Up until now, in spite of troublesome episodes, we had made good progress, but the election of 2006 turned the table. Ward C and D seats were up for election. The conservative recruiters found Pat Steel to run against Nancy Dowdy in Ward C, and Lorie Smith ran against Reo Hatfield in Ward D.

George Hartsook, a low-rent property owner in Waynesboro, loosely organized a Stuarts Draft political action committee that he named the American Property Owners Association. It was formed primarily to support candidates who would combat any plans to use taxpayer money to help pay for renovations to the Wayne Theatre.

The Wayne Theater was built in 1926 by two residents, Colonels Loth and Patterson, as a vaudeville and silent movie venue. Over the years, it morphed into a traditional movie theater, and in 2000, the business closed, and the historic building was given to the city.

A group of volunteer citizens interested in the arts organized the Wayne Theatre Alliance (WTA) with a mission to rehabilitate the theater and create a community performance venue. In September of 2001, City Council loaned them $29,000 to pay a consultant to study the feasibility of their plans. The City handed the theater building over to the Economic Development Association with the intention of eventually deeding it to the WTA if and when the organization met certain developmental goals. The WTA membership frequently lobbied City Council for money to renovate the theater. Many of Waynesboro's residents, including Hartsook, were opposed to the city giving taxpayer money to the WTA for the renovations. Council candidates Hatfield and Steele were among them.

Hartsook perpetrated a voter bribery scandal by posting fliers on the windshields of cars in T-Bone

Jack's parking lot: "VOTE Hatfield and Steele and WIN! WIN! WIN!" It was an offer to enter the names of those who promised to vote for Hatfield and Steele into a drawing. A variety of prizes valued at a total of $2,000 included a free session at a nail salon and up to $500 cash. On Friday, April 28, *The News Virginian* reported that Hatfield and Steele disavowed any connection to the fliers or the American Property Owners Association or its president, George Hartsook.

There was a state police investigation into Hartsook's actions. A judge ordered him to pay a $250 fine on the misdemeanor charges springing from the scandal. A pair of suspended, 10-day jail stints accompanied the fine. It was thought that he meant no harm and was basically clueless when it came to politics.

It was no secret that I was campaigning for Hatfield and Steele. On the day before the election, the paper carried an editorial headlined "Don't Let One Man Decide Our Election."

The puppet master pulling the strings of the Waynesboro City Council election is not George Hartsook....It's not the two Augusta men—Leroy Wilkinson and Dave Wolfe— running Pat Steele's campaign against incumbent Nancy Dowdy....No, the real force behind this election is a sitting Councilman who has never been elected to anything.

Todd Foster, the editor was referring to the fact that I had been appointed to my seat on Council. In the same editorial, Foster made a very damaging allegation accusing Hatfield and me of a backroom deal.

Lorie Smith, Hatfield's opponent, was a well-spoken, pleasant-seeming life-long resident. Foster's editorial accused me of trying to convince Smith to step down from the race: "Smith says Lucente asked her not to run against Hatfield. 'Let Hatfield win,' he said, 'then Hatfield will be elected mayor but resign in two years.' Lucente promised Smith that she would be appointed to Hatfield's vacant seat. Smith said no way."

Backroom political deals are unethical, to say the least. This conversation between Smith and me never happened, and I was duty-bound to clear my name. I called her up and recorded our conversation. She denied telling the paper that I had offered her a deal. Then I called the TV station and told them that Smith had confirmed on tape that the paper's accusations were false. They said they would have to hear it from her directly.

But Smith wouldn't talk to the TV station. The following morning, Election Day, I took my administrative assistant with me to act as a witness and went to see Foster's boss, Bruce Potter, publisher of *The News Virginian*. We talked in his conference room. I told him that I wasn't accusing anyone specific, but that somebody was lying, and I needed to get to the bottom of this. I told him that Smith had denied making the accusation, and I turned on the tape of the previous morning's phone conversation where she clearly stated, "I didn't say that, Frank."

> "I didn't say that, Frank."

Potter asked warily if I was recording my conversation with him also. He said that the paper had a tape of their interview with Smith and that he would check it for accuracy. It was a few hours later when Potter got back to me. He said his findings showed that we were both wrong and both right, but offered no explanation of exactly what he meant by that. I demanded that he retract the accusation in an editorial, but that was never done to my satisfaction. On the editorial page on Wednesday, May 3, 2006, the day after the election, a correction appeared under the inexplicit headline "Excerpt from the Lorie Smith interview":

Lorie Smith interviewed with *The News Virginian* editorial board on April 18. An editorial Monday misstated the identity of the Councilman who Lorie Smith says told her Reo Hatfield would only serve two years of his term if re-elected, and that he would support her for the open seat. This misstatement was not brought to our attention until Tuesday.

This audio-to-text transcription of the interview followed:

Mr. Hatfield told me back in January that he was going to spend whatever it took to beat DuBose Egleston—back in December, rather—because they had heard that I was getting ready to announce my candidacy. I had several conversations with these guys trying to get me not to run—essentially.

One was right here in this building. In this building! Frank Lucente, the night that y'all had your open house [Nov. 1], he pulled me down the hallway back there and said, "You know that Mr. Hat…that Reo is going to run."

I said, "That's wonderful."

He said, "I'm hearing rumors that you're going to run."

I said, "Frank, to be quite honest with you, I have not made a decision."

And Reo talked to me. And Reo said basically, I am going to run and I don't want to run against you. And simply if you will just wait two years, I'll put my resources behind you and get you elected in two years because I am not going to serve out another four-year term.

I said to myself at that point, if I ever was indecisive about running, at that point, and knew that someone was coming in for a four-year term and wasn't going to spend but two years of it, there was something wrong with this picture.

Smith beat Hatfield, and I sued the paper for a million dollars for defamation of character. It was the only time I've ever sued anybody, and it wasn't about the money. If I had won, the money would have been donated to the Boys & Girls Club.

I couldn't find a local attorney who could represent me. A number of those I approached had a connection to the paper. Wayne Heslep in nearby Lexington, Virginia, took my case. A big headline on the front page of the Waynesboro paper read "Councilman Sues Paper," and then they offered me a settlement of $5,000.

I turned down the offer. I was taking this to trial! I wanted the public to see what the paper had done. But Judge Humes Franklin issued a demurrer, which in effect dismissed the case on the grounds that even if the facts alleged in the complaint were true, which was not disputed, there was no legal basis for the lawsuit. I strongly disagreed. In my mind, the paper offering me a settlement was bribery, an admission of wrongdoing. I wanted to take my case on to the Supreme Court.

Heslep explained to me that only about five percent of cases are overturned in the Supreme Court. He advised that my case could be viewed as just politics and thrown out. He filed the briefs and the two of us went together to Richmond to present our case. Heslep was right. My case was seen as just politics and went nowhere, but I am glad to have stood my ground.

Potter was removed from the staff of *The News Virginian*, transferred to some other paper in the chain. Before long, Foster was also transferred. A conservative journalist, Lee Wolverton took over the paper. He confirmed that I was right all along saying, "Frank, you had us by the balls."

My actions completely changed the landscape at *The News Virginian*. I lost the battle but won the war. Wolverton's leadership brought a much less

Smith unseats Hatfield

Dowdy defeats Steele

By ALICIA PETSKA
apetska@newsvirginian.com

For the first time in Waynesboro history, two women will be sitting on City Council. Nancy Dowdy and Lorie Smith both claimed election victories, taking down about 56 percent and 49 percent of the vote, respectively.

"We keep breaking ground, and I think that's wonderful," Dowdy said from her home, where she was hosting a victory party. ... This has restored my faith in the people of Waynesboro, that they care about more than the tax rate."

Tuesday's vote marked the close of a negative campaign, one for the record books, according to some. At the Waynesboro Country Club, where her friends and supporters had gathered, Smith said her reaction to the news of her victory was "tears."

See **SMITH**, Page A6

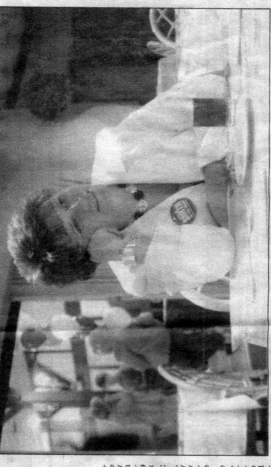

Lorie Smith takes a moment to reflect on winning the Ward D seat in Tuesday's Waynesboro City Council election. Smith's supporters gathered at the Waynesboro Country Club.

NATHAN COHRS/Staff

The News Virginian, May 3, 2006

political approach to the paper's reporting. He told me that a suit of this nature would have cost the paper $100,000. It had cost me $30,000.

Hartsook faded into the woodwork. While writing this chapter, I called Hatfield to ask for the first time if he had perhaps suggested to Smith that she not run. He said the reports were not accurate, that words were taken out of context. He thinks he might have jokingly made a suggestion in passing. Maybe this is what Potter meant by both wrong and right. Maybe he heard on the tape that the deal was offered to Smith, just not by me.

CHAPTER 5

The Minority Years

Being a minority player on Council can be advantageous in some ways and brought out the best in me. I drew less attention doing research and was able to present comparison views that often produced a better outcome.

Our local elections are held on the first Tuesday of May and the newly elected officials take office on July 1. Nancy Dowdy retained her seat in 2006, and Lorie Smith took Reo Hatfield's seat. The first meeting in July, as directed by the City Code, is an organizational meeting. The floor is opened to nominations for Mayor. Dowdy moved to nominate Tom Reynolds, and Smith seconded the nomination. He was elected unanimously in a show of solidarity, and Dowdy was voted in as Vice Mayor, also unanimously. A nay vote wouldn't have changed the outcome anyhow because the majority rules. These three people were the new majority, and they were going to run things for the next two years.

There is a vote to appoint or re-appoint the city's four charter appointments, those staff positions overseen by Council. Then Council members are assigned to committees based on their interests and skills. This is where I learned quickly what it was going to be like on the minority side. I was pulled off of the Planning Committee and the Finance Committee. Instead, in a short-sighted move, I was relegated to the Flood Control Committee, a do-nothing group that didn't meet a single time during my two-year assignment.

Finance is my great interest and my strong suit! Those who know me have heard me express over and over again my belief that this country is in serious trouble because genuinely qualified people do not step up to run for public office. In order for the citizens to be effectively served, we must elect local officials who respect and understand money and budget. Here I was, a very willing and qualified Councilman, but my relevant skills were side-stepped.

A Councilman's primary job is to set tax rates, allocate tax dollars for the common good of the community, and prevent unnecessary tax increases. I support providing essential services that make the city a viable, safe, and healthy place to live: police and fire protection, public education, maintenance of roads and parks, water and sewage management, stormwater management, and economic develop-ment. That's about it. But privileged people repeated-ly line up holding their hands out for public money while needy people wouldn't think of it.

Case in point: The small Waynesboro Heritage Museum on the corner of Wayne and Main is a non-profit. It is housed in a restored bank building that's owned by the city's Housing Authority. It is operated by a foundation that is governed by a

Finance is... my strong suit!

Board of Directors. The foundation also manages the historic Plumb House, which is owned by the city. The Plumb House was built around 1802. It has been home to five generations of Plumbs and is the oldest frame dwelling in Waynesboro. It weathered the Civil War Battle of Waynesboro and has a cannonball embedded in its framework. The museum displays collections of Civil War and Native American artifacts. I personally am an enthusiastic private contributor and member of the foundation.

Since 2005, the city had been granting $22,500 per year to the Heritage Museum, and city employees were providing upkeep for the Plumb House. In 2007, City Council passed a resolution to honor Shirley Bridgeforth, the volunteer director and heart and soul of the Heritage Museum. The resolution described her "remarkable achievement in the furtherance of making the City of Waynesboro more mindful of its rich history and heritage."

Heritage Museum, 2018

In the fall of 2007, at Bridgeforth's request, the majority of Council voted to increase that year's grant by an additional $7,123. It was to be a one-time increase to pay for publishing *The History of Waynesboro 1900–1976* written by historian and retired DuPont engineer, George Hawke.

Mayor Reynolds was very much in favor of using taxpayer money for this purpose. He felt it was time for Waynesboro to get some attention. Chris Graham, blogger and owner of the *Augusta Free Press,* quotes Reynolds as saying, "...Waynesboro has a heritage that has been kept under a bushel basket for years....Certain that the city should not be in the museum business or the book business, I opposed the increase. Even Hawke agreed with me, but the increase which brought the museum's funding to a total of $29,623 was passed on a 3–2 vote. Reynolds, Dowdy, and Smith in favor, Williams and I opposed. (Hawke's book is for sale in the museum's gift shop for $49.99 but not on Amazon.)

Later that winter, I was invited to a dinner at the museum. It was an attempt to sway my thinking about donating city funds to the museum. Bridgeforth and volunteers in period costumes served the food and made their pitch. They wanted the city to contribute $180,000 per year so that they could hire a curator and expand the program. They justified their request by positioning the museum as an educational and economic development instrument for Waynesboro.

They told me that the museum had about 3,000 visitors the previous year. I knew that many of those were repeat visitors. I did the math and pointed out that they were asking the city for about $60 of taxpayer funds per visitor. This is not a government thing! Why would they expect the public, most of whom never stepped foot into the museum, to bear the costs? I told them I would not support their request.

In the spring of 2008, in a 2009 budget work session, Mayor Reynolds asked Council to increase the museum's grant by an additional $30,000 so that they could hire a Director. Dowdy and Smith were in favor. So, in a matter of months, the taxpayer contribution to the Heritage Museum climbed from $22,500 to $29,623 to cover the book, then to $59,500, and there was nothing I could do about it.

Bridgeforth used the city's money to turn her volunteer position into a paid position. I was having lunch with the Assistant City Manager one day when she walked past the window. "There goes a city employee," he said. "[Bridgeforth] pays herself with city money, but there's no requirement for accountability."

While doing the research for this book, I learned that the one-time increase for Hawke's book continued to stay in the budget year after year. No one noticed, including me! Of course, the museum staff knew, but they never brought it up, and there was no obligation for the museum to report on how any of the city's money was spent.

In 2008, Mayor Reynolds retired, and Bruce Allen filled his seat on Council. The new make-up of Council was more conservative, and we went about the business of incrementally reducing the funding allotted to the museum. In 2010, it was cut back to $48,500. In 2011–2012, it was cut back to $30,000. In 2013, it

No one noticed, including me!

was cut back to $27,500, which is where it remains today. Reports in 2017, show that visitation to the museum is now down to about 1,750 per year. With today's allotment, that's a taxpayer subsidy of about $15.75 per visitor.

During 2016, my last year in office, I tried to get it reduced some more but was told by a fellow Councilman to let it ride. He said there was an effort underway to have a much larger museum located in Waynesboro and further reduction would look as if the city did not support its local museum. I stood my ground and voted against passing that year's budget, but the $27,500 still goes to the Heritage Museum. State funding for the larger museum never happened.

Over a dozen years, the city granted the museum more than $400,000. And the taxpayers know nothing about any of this! Of course, it appeared in the complex city budget document, but generally, that isn't something the public sees—$400,000 here, $400,000 there, it starts to look like some real money. This sort of thing happens all the time. The Heritage Museum is a treasured establishment in Waynesboro deserving of the community's support and mine personally. But I feel that CAPSAW is the suitable funding resource, not the city treasury.

CHAPTER 6

The Wayne Theatre

On Monday afternoon, April 23, 2007, I went into City Manager Doug Walker's office to get my briefing on the agenda for that evening's bi-weekly City Council meeting. It seemed like a run-of-the-mill meeting: an award to be given, closure of a city street for a muscle car show, presentation by the transportation safety commission, a pay compensation study, and appropriation ordinances. After a casual chat, I asked if there was anything else I should know before that night's meeting. Walker said, "There is nothing else that I know of."

That evening, things proceeded pretty much as expected until Mayor Reynolds introduced an ordinance about transferring some leftover money from the regional jail and Health Department funds into the general reserve fund. What unfolded was like a well-rehearsed performance. Reynolds then stated that it would be appropriate to use these funds to meet the requirements of City Code § 98-384. The Code reads, "Owners of historic landmarks or historic contributing buildings and structures shall not allow them to fall into a state of disrepair so as to endanger their physical integrity or the public health or safety."

Reynolds was in favor of giving the Wayne Theatre to the Economic Development Authority (EDA) for transfer to the Wayne Theatre Alliance (WTA), but that had not yet occurred, and he was now citing the city's legal responsibility as the current owner of the building to maintain the integrity of the structure. He stated that if the roof of the Wayne Theatre was not repaired soon, the structural integrity of the building would certainly fail. He suggested that Council not introduce the ordinance he had just read. Instead, he recommended that Council instruct staff to prepare a different ordinance to introduce at the next meeting. The new ordinance would appropriate $300,000 to the EDA to assist with repairing the roof of the Wayne Theatre building. This, he said, was in order to expedite the transfer of the property to the EDA. He also stated that this was "found money," a statement that he would come to regret because of public outcry.

Like clockwork, Dowdy chimed in that she fully supported the Mayor's recommendation. She stated that it would cost the city $300,000 just to tear down the building, and it couldn't be done right away because of its historical designation. Then, Smith agreed that it would be appropriate to use the leftover money since it would not affect the 2008 budget. In addition to the proposed ordinance, she asked Council to consider an agreement stipulating that "other money" also be passed along to the EDA for the Wayne Theatre in a timely

Williams and I were blindsided.

fashion, recognizing that Council cannot legally bind the actions or spending of future Councils.

And that was that. Those three Council members made up the majority and they were going to give the EDA $300,000, which would be passed on to the Wayne Theatre Alliance.

Williams and I were blindsided and asked for clarification as to what action we were being asked to take. Mayor Reynolds stated that the only action from Council would be a consensus to instruct staff to prepare the new ordinance for consideration at Council's next meeting. My response to the Mayor's proposal was that this was all a surprise to me. It was the first time that I had heard anything about this!

Even when I was a majority Councilman, I would never have brought up something during a Council meeting that I had not previously shared with Council or staff. No one likes to be caught off guard in a public meeting and everyone knew my position on this courtesy. It had happened before when Dowdy flipped on First Bank's request for a curb cut.

Williams and I were blindsided not only by our fellow Council members but also by the City Manager. He was a big supporter of the Wayne Theatre, openly pushing for the city to support it in any way possible. It is Council's job to set policy, not the City Manager's. Whether or not to give taxpayer money to the Wayne Theatre is a policy issue. Walker had crossed a line. He had actively colluded with the majority of Council members, deliberately excluding Williams and me from their decision to contribute money to the theater. We were given no opportunity to research the issue or even gather our thoughts. I knew then that if I ever had the opportunity, I would vote to replace Walker with a new City Manager.

Smith, Dowdy, and Reynolds had voiced their decisions. Williams and I did the best we could under the circumstances to reiterate our unwavering stand against the use of taxpayer money for private interest, but it was a waste of time. This was a done deal before the two of us knew anything about it. Smith made the motion to introduce an ordinance at our next meeting to give $300,000 to the EDA to repair the roof for the WTA. Dowdy seconded the motion with the addition of instructions to establish directions for Council regarding future funding for the Wayne Theatre. The motion passed 3–2; Smith, Dowdy and Reynolds in favor, Williams and I opposed. So, $300,000 of taxpayer money was on its way out, just like that.

One week later, on April 30, 2007, there was a Public Hearing to reassess property taxes. In spite of this not being a regular Council meeting, a resolution was presented giving the WTA $300,000 immediately and another $700,000 over ten years. This was the "other money" Smith wanted the resolution to cover. Following nine clauses that start with the word WHEREAS, the resolution includes:

NOW, THEREFORE, BE IT RESOLVED, that the Waynesboro City Council intends to allocate $300,000 in economic development incentive funds as an initial contribution to the Economic Development Authority of the City of Waynesboro for the identified purpose of promoting economic development, specifically earmarked for the Wayne Theatre project...

AND BE IT RESOLVED FURTHER that the City Council of the City of Waynesboro pledges future contributions to the Wayne Theatre over a period of not more than ten (10) years in a total amount of $700,000, as valued presently, through future allocations of economic development incentive funds to the Economic Development Authority, as such funds are identified appropriate by City Council...

Wayne Theater, 2018

AND BE IT RESOLVED FURTHER that transfers of all funds in excess of the specific FY2007 funds contemplated herein [the $300,000] shall be conditioned upon the Waynesboro Economic Development Authority successfully entering into a performance-based agreement and incentive structure with the Wayne Theatre Alliance, LLC...

Dowdy moved adoption of the resolution, and Smith seconded the motion. Anticipating this, I had prepared the following statement to read at the Public Hearing:

As we propose another resolution for funding the Wayne Theatre, I wanted to reiterate my position on the issue of funding and my reasons for that position. First of all, let me say, I am personally in support of the Wayne Theatre and was happy to donate money to the Wayne Theatre Alliance. However, personal feelings are not the issue here, but what makes sense for all the citizens of Waynesboro and funding the Wayne Theatre with public funds does not. I say this for three principled reasons.

First, I do not believe the City should be a funder of any private incentive initiatives on this level, and the Council seemed to agree with me when we voted 5–0 not to be the primary funder of such initiatives. You can argue what primary means, but when the City is planning to give $1 million to private enterprise, in my mind, we are a primary funder.

Second, I do not believe the business plan put forward by the Wayne Theatre Alliance is sound. Much of the plan and the proposed benefit to the city is [sic] based on what I consider overly optimistic estimates. For example, their plan projects they will sell 50,000 tickets per year. That is nearly 1,000 tickets per week. They further project $75,000 per year in revenue to the city. Closer examination of the plan shows that two-thirds of that revenue is from nearly 10,000 overnight visitors. That is 200 per week. So, their plan is based on 1,000 tickets sold and 200 overnight visitors per week, 52 weeks per year. As much as I would like to believe these estimates are accurate and they could fill this plan, I am not willing to gamble with the taxpayers' money on them.

Finally, a lot has been said about the quality of life in Waynesboro and how this investment in the theater will improve our quality of life. I would like to point out the improvement in the quality of life that has happened in Waynesboro over the last four years since the City Council began lowering the tax rate. We moved from last to first in the region in sales tax revenues, added dozens of new businesses, and we have two new shopping centers and over 800 new homes under development in the city. Waynesboro is thriving and our efficient government and low taxes are a big part of that. We are not like the other cities in Virginia or even in our region that are suffering economic slowdowns and reductions in revenue. We are just the opposite, and we should continue on our path. The only way to keep taxes low and continue the path of growth we started is to manage our city finances conservatively and efficiently. We should not make large investments in private initiatives, especially where the business plan and the benefit to the city are so speculative. Lower taxes not only bring business and ultimately added revenue to the city, but low taxes are part of the reason people move to and stay in Waynesboro.

Thank you.

The citizens who had gathered for the Public Hearing clapped and cheered me on, but the resolution was passed 3–2 with booing and other sounds of disparagement coming from the audience.

After the Public Hearing, I reminded the City Manager that Council cannot give money through a resolution. According to the City Code, it has to come from an ordinance. So, it was introduced by Smith as an ordinance at our next regularly scheduled Council meeting on May 14 and voted on at the next Council meeting on May 29, 2007, with the expected 3–2 outcome. Even with the four-week delay I imposed, it was still all wrapped up in five weeks.

This got the ball rolling. The EDA composed an agreement stipulating that if the WTA met specific goals they would receive periodic draws on the $700,000 from the city through the EDA, providing the sitting City Council was willing. That left the big unavoidable question: Would future Councils dole out this money?

The $300,000 was given directly to the WTA with no requirement for measures of accountability. It was years later after the building was transferred to them that the roof repairs and other improvements occurred.

I always wondered about the sudden rush to get that money. I learned later that the state had offered a $500,000 grant if the WTA could raise funds to match that gift within a specific time frame. Time was running out, and they had only raised $200,000. Three members of Council pushed the rest through for them.

In early 2008, the EDA sought Council's approval for the performance agreement they had been charged with crafting. Titled the Wayne Theatre Incentive Package, it stated the EDA would grant another $200,000 to the WTA when they received

This got the ball rolling.

their certificate of occupancy, which was expected to occur in 2009. The WTA was required to produce twelve major events per year and spend $50,000 on advertising and promotions per year. The agreement would be in place for a maximum of 10 years, and if the contingencies were met, the WTA would receive a grant each year until the $700,000 ran out.

Smith commended the EDA for their good work, and Dowdy moved to adopt a pre-arranged resolution. It read in part as follows:

> WHEREAS the EDA undertook its assignment from City Council and has submitted a proposed performance agreement for the

responsible administration of the Wayne Theatre Incentive Package: and

WHEREAS, the City Council, upon mature consideration and review of such performance agreement, has determined that the EDA has diligently and capably responded to its charge from City Council, and has negotiated, authorized, and presented a performance agreement to the City Council that will (i) accomplish the intent of the Wayne Theatre Incentive Package as approved by City Council, (ii) protect the interests of the City, and (iii) incentivize successful economic development activity in the downtown....

AND BE IT RESOLVED FURTHER that the City Council hereby approves, confirms, and ratifies its intent to fund, in full, the $700,000 Wayne Theatre Incentive Package as valued presently, over a period not to exceed ten years and in increments of sufficient size and regularity for the EDA to administer the annual incentive grants enumerated in the Performance Agreement.

AND BE IT RESOLVED FURTHER that nothing herein is intended to limit any future action on the part of the Waynesboro City Council regarding allocation of economic development incentive funds to the Waynesboro Economic Development Authority for this or any other project, specified or unspecified.

That last paragraph is very important to understand. The City Code states that a sitting Council cannot commit money on behalf of future Councils. So, this is a non-binding resolution, meaning future Councils can act on it or not, as they choose.

I went on record as reiterating my faith in the EDA, saying that the agreement was well done. But I wanted to be very clear that I would not vote in favor of the resolution, nor would I support giving the Wayne Theatre any of the taxpayers' money as long I was elected to Council. With no further comments, the resolution passed with the expected 3–2 vote.

Council changes every two years, and in 2008, when Allen took Reynolds's seat, the majority shifted and brought a different attitude toward money for the theater. As I write this in the winter of 2018, none of the $700,000 has been granted to them. Of course, that could change at any time.

No other issue in my 11 years on Council brought out the people the way the Wayne Theatre controversy did. The WTA worked hard to get the theater up and running with other resources, an enormous accomplishment in my opinion. They still push for city money because their business plan is inadequate, and they will always need donated money to sustain the operations. They imply that a promise has been broken, but a non-binding resolution is <u>not</u> a promise. It's up to Waynesboro's taxpayers to stay involved and direct the spending of city money as they see fit.

CHAPTER 7

The Election of 2008

The 2006–2008 minority years were contentious. Important issues usually resulted in a 3–2 vote, with Williams and me on the losing end. Mayor Tom Reynolds decided not to run for a third term in 2008. Williams and I ran. Whether from contentment or just indifference on the part of the voters, Williams ran unopposed for the third time, once for the School Board and twice for Council. I had opposition from Jeremy Taylor, an elected School Board member and attorney, as well as the perennial Dubose Egleston.

The conservative recruiters searched for someone to run in ward B, the seat Tom Reynolds was vacating. We didn't have much luck until a friend of mine, Lloyd Holloway, suggested Bruce Allen. Allen was a retired city sheriff and a lifelong city resident. He shared my interest in the Boys & Girls Club and is its longest serving board member. He volunteers for the Salvation Army and is a Mason, a Shriner, a member of the F.O.P., and a board member for the Soap Box Derby. He belongs to the Elks, Moose, and Lions Clubs. He hadn't missed a Lions Club meeting in 10 years. I ask him to run for Council, and after some consideration, he agreed to it.

Campaign sign

He was opposed by Greg Bruno who had an online news website and a seat on the city's Planning Commission. His other opponent was Chris Graham, the very active blogger who focused on local news and politics for his *Augusta Free Press*.

A group of political activists worked with Allen to drum up support. He and I had been casual friends for years and shared conservative views when it came to money. We ran separate campaigns, but he pushed his supporters to vote for me, and I pushed hard for him.

Graham was also a lifelong resident, and he was a UVA graduate. He was highly visible in the community, a social media expert who was endorsed by *The News Virginian*, where he had once worked. I spoke with Graham after a council meeting and told him it looked to me as if he was going to win. I said I hoped we'd have a chance to work together, but inside I was worried that he would support the Wayne Theatre's incessant requests for taxpayer money.

This was my first campaign since running for the state House of Delegates in West Virginia 24 years earlier. I had a lot of supporters in Waynesboro, but I was opposed by numerous special interest groups who were vying for taxpayer money. Nonetheless, I felt that my experience with campaigning gave me a big advantage over my opponents. After all, there were only four precincts in Waynesboro compared to the 80 precincts I had to cover in West Virginia. I reasoned that the smaller population would allow me to run a grassroots campaign, actually connecting to all the voters.

There were approximately 11,000 registered voters in Waynesboro in 2008, but history showed that only about 3,000 would turn out to vote. Fifteen hundred votes would mean a big win, leaving the other 1,500 to be split between my two opponents.

I set up a campaign committee that consisted of 15 volunteer generals who would each have 10 volunteer lieutenants working for them. That's 150 volunteers working on my campaign. The lieutenants would each recruit 10 people to vote for me. I pushed each volunteer to honor his or her commitment, which included making sure that their voters came out to vote. That would produce the necessary 1,500 votes.

We met every ten days or so and kept a chart that showed good progress from week to week. I ran the standard newspaper ads and had brochures printed. I also had high-quality silk-screened campaign signs made locally. I chose a white background with lime green lettering, and I painted my signposts to match the lettering so they really stood out.

I attended all the local political meetings and debates. Working harder on this than on anything else in my life caused me so much stress that I developed a mild case of shingles. Campaigning is all about how many people you can get to follow you. I am a firm believer that it's not the better man who wins the election. It's the one who works the hardest and has the greater sense of the issues that matter to the voters. Something I like about this process is that you either win or lose. There are no grey areas. I had a good feeling as the campaign progressed, but one's own perspective can be misleading.

Taylor, one of my opponents, was on the School Board, but he worked in Charlottesville and did not have the community connections that I had. Egleston ran in every election and had a small base that did not seem to be much of a threat. The voters had seen me in action as an appointed Councilman. They knew me and knew that I had the entire community's best interest at heart.

Allen and I campaigned vigorously against giving taxpayer money to the Wayne Theatre. We felt certain that the general public was against it, but some of the city's movers and shakers were working hard to gain support for the theater's funding requests.

In my history of running for office, I had never sought favor for or received an endorsement from a special interest group. Not a single union or political action committee, not public employees, or any other group who might endorse their preferred candidate. It's an unfortunate system that promotes endorsement of candidates who will bring some benefit to the group who endorses them.

We certainly did not solicit it, but the Invista union workers in Waynesboro threw their support to Allen and me. The Invista management was upset that the city was considering instituting a stormwater fee that would cost Invista upwards of $200,000 per year. Invista had bought the DuPont plant in Waynesboro and was competing with China in the Lycra business and working on close margins. They already had stormwater infrastructure in place and thought this fee was very unfair. So, they asked their union to support Allen and me because we were also opposed to the stormwater fee as it was being proposed at that time.

Many of the approximately 300 Invista employees lived outside the city and were not eligible to vote in the city election, and many who were eligible were not registered. The union went to work on our behalf to get their qualifying members registered.

Early in the campaign, Mayor Reynolds, who was close to the end of his term, stated that he was not going to endorse any candidates for Council seats. He thought that would be out of line for a sitting Mayor. So, we were caught off guard when his letter endorsing Taylor showed up in the voters' mailboxes on the Wednesday before the Tuesday election.

My campaign committee met to consider the situation, and I told them that I felt it was too late to respond to the letter of endorsement. They didn't agree with me. They thought that if I could hastily get a letter written and printed they could address the envelopes and get a response in the mail to voters by the Thursday or Friday before the Tuesday election.

> **We were caught off guard.**

We went to work. I had previously purchased the state list of all the local people who had voted in the last six elections, approximately 2,500. I composed two letters, one for newly registered voters and one for long-time voters.

On Wednesday, April 30, the letters were printed on lime green stationery, and I was all set for when the committee would arrive at 11:00 a.m. to address the envelopes. Then I received word that my daughter Emily was at the maternity ward in labor, so I headed to the hospital instead. I left the list of voters at the meeting room and called a key committee worker to let him know what was going on.

Lila Jane Stevens, my granddaughter, was born at 1:00 p.m. Once I'd seen her beautiful face and knew that everything was okay, I headed for the meeting room fearful that the mailing opportunity had been lost. The unexpected assembly line of about 20 people addressing envelopes was one of the greatest and most humbling of my Council experiences. At the sight of those dedicated supporters, I knew I was going to win.

And I did win and win big! The voter turnout was 29.2 percent, better than expected, and the count was 1,996 votes for me and 800 for Jeremy Taylor and 518 for Dubose Egleston. A pleasant surprise was that Bruce Allen also won by a landslide.

Votes by ward

Waynesboro City Council *100% of precincts reporting*

WARD B	A	B	C	D	Total
Bruce Allen	248	617	351	770	2,030
Greg Bruno	37	150	48	132	377
Chris Graham	35	339	91	375	869
AT-LARGE	A	B	C	D	Total
DuBose Egleston	53	197	80	172	518
Frank Lucente (I)	231	616	339	770	1,996
Jeremy Taylor	31	308	77	357	800

Staunton *100% of precincts reporting*

CITY COUNCIL	1	2	3	4	5	Total
Rusty Ashby	216	351	310	340	165	1,434
Richard Bell (I)	299	551	441	469	263	2,081
Bob Campbell	280	463	332	264	159	1,537
Ophie Kier	345	545	463	495	415	2,347
David Metz (I)	219	399	338	459	354	1,832
Andrea Oakes	225	381	347	355	225	1,582
SCHOOL BOARD	1	2	3	4	5	Total
George Ballew	254	395	377	375	227	1,686
Sarah Crenshaw	290	491	416	368	225	1,851
John Hart	221	327	255	230	156	1,230
Daniel Stuhlsatz	164	316	289	329	261	1,412
Write-in*	66	147	116	183	158	698

*Ron Ramsey (I) ran as write-in candidate.
I – Incumbent. Totals include absentee ballots.

He received 2,030 votes, Chris Graham had 869, and Greg Bruno had 377. Tim Williams also got a substantial vote of 2,424 considering that usually in uncontested races very few people bother to vote. It was the biggest win in a Waynesboro City Council election in recent memory.

The losing parties attributed their losses to our Invista endorsement. But after the election, I checked the new registrations, and there had been no more than 25 voters registered between the time the union encouraged employees to register and the deadline. I estimate the endorsement garnered us each about 50 votes.

At-large City Councilman Frank Lucente talks on the phone Tuesday while campaigning at Westminster Presbyterian Church.

The News Virginian, May 7, 2008

My campaign committee and my campaign strategy had worked like a charm. Allen's long-term commitment to the community through volunteer work and his determined campaigning had paid off in spades. Allen, Williams, and I felt confident that our victories meant we were doing what the people wanted. Two arduous years of being in the minority were finally over. I was back in the majority!

ROSANNE WEBER/STAFF

Bruce Allen, right, celebrates alongside Tim Williams and Frank Lucente, left, after winning the Ward B seat on the Waynesboro City Council on Tuesday night.

Lucente savors big night

CHAPTER 8

A Matter of Code

As soon as the election was over, and before the new Council took office, Williams and I turned our attention to Douglas Walker. He had been the City Manager since 2003, before I was appointed to Council. He was an intelligent and ambitious young man with a magnetic personality. He was well liked and respected by his co-workers. He could juggle numerous projects at once, and it was a challenge to keep up with him.

As I've said, the City Code states that the Council sets policy, and the City Manager carries out policy and operates the city. Walker overstepped the bounds of his position when it came to policy, manipulating the Council in order to carry out his own agenda. In 2007, I had noticed workers and equipment from the Public Works Department being used to help remove debris from the Wayne Theatre. I called Walker on it, and first thing you know, a resolution to allow Public Works to do that sort of thing appeared before Council and was passed on a 3–2 vote. At that time, it was Reynolds, Smith, and Dowdy in favor; Williams and I opposed.

I guess it was understandable that Walker was a strong supporter of the theater because his wife was a talented singer. He remained a firm believer that city government should help the Wayne Theatre Alliance (WTA). I hadn't trusted him since the night he blindsided us with the $300,000 donation to repair the theater roof. I once advised him that if he wanted to set policy for the city, he needed to run for a Council seat. Some of his staff and I cautioned that he was treading on dangerous ground, but he kept on.

I liked him personally and enjoyed his company, but that did not sway me when it came to my public duties. Williams and Hatfield had thought Walker was overstepping his bounds and wanted to replace him back in 2005 when I was first appointed to Council. But I had not yet witnessed his job performance and wanted to give him a chance. Now back in the majority, I was ready to have him replaced.

When Allen won the election, Williams and I asked him if he would consider not renewing Walker's contract. He said he would go along with us. Walker had never talked with Allen during the election campaign. It was clear that he thought Graham would win and join Dowdy and Smith in granting public funds to the WTA. I give Allen a great deal of credit for taking our word about Walker. I couldn't have blamed him for wanting to get to know him first, as I had chosen to do when first on Council.

The three of us decided that Williams would ask for Walker's resignation, and we informed Dowdy and Smith of our decision. We would let him resign rather than fire him. That would look better on his résumé. Walker made a call to Allen looking for support, but Allen told him that he would not support a reappointment. I informed Walker that I would not support his reappointment either. It would only take the three of us Councilmen to force his resignation.

> **I was ready to have him replaced.**

At the regular business meeting of May 27, 2008, Council went into a closed session to formalize the decision. When the open session immediately resumed, Walker presented an expansive letter of resignation that included the following closing statement:

The time has come for me to transition to the next chapter in my career. I do so with the hope and trust that together with City Council and city staff, I have contributed some measure of the "right stuff" that makes for a better Waynesboro today, and that will help Waynesboro continue to be a first-class community for the next generation of citizens.

Dowdy was prepared with this statement:

One of my first responsibilities as a newly elected official almost six years ago was the honor of hiring a new City Manager....

Many terms come to mind when I reflect on Mr. Walker's tenure, but two stand out the most.

First is leadership as defined by James MacGregor Burns: "...the genius of leadership lies in the manner in which leaders see and act on their own and their followers' values and motivations."

Second is integrity. It is Mr. Walker's upstanding and unwavering integrity that has brought us where we are tonight.

She then expressed her gratitude for what she saw as the 39 high-points of his career in Waynesboro and ended by saying she was at a loss as to why Council was going in this direction. Smith followed suit with praise for his leadership and accomplishments. Mayor Reynolds made the following statement:

> I have been on Council eight years, and June 30th is my last day, and this is the toughest thing I am going to have to do. Tonight, ladies and gentlemen, I am going to "fall on my sword" for Doug Walker. As much as I do not want to accept his resignation, I must so that Doug can leave with dignity and respect that he's earned in these six years that he has served Waynesboro so admirably. And it is a shame, especially when a newly elected Council member has never even taken the opportunity to come and talk to Doug about anything. How can you make an informed decision if you don't even talk to the person you have an issue with?

And so, he voted with Williams and me in favor of accepting Walker's resignation. Smith and Dowdy were opposed. It was a done deal.

Part of the blame for this happening lay at the feet of Smith, Dowdy, and Reynolds who failed to inform all the members of the previous Council of their intentions regarding WTA funding.

Walker and I had a history of good discussions, and we had agreed on many things. One very constructive accomplishment stands out. Separating the water, sewage, and garbage businesses from the general fund and having them function on their independent revenues was of significant benefit to the city. His online LinkedIn résumé says this about his professional years in Waynesboro:

City Manager
City of Waynesboro, Virginia
January 2003–July 2008 (5 years 7 months)
Served as the chief administrative officer in a council—manager form of government for an independent municipality providing a full range of services to a growing community of 20,000+, with 340 full-time staff, and a total budget of approximately $71 million, including water, sewer, and solid waste enterprise funds. Specific municipal services for which responsible included finance (accounts receivable, accounts payable, utility billing, payroll, risk

management, audit); budget (development and management, capital improvement plan, purchasing and inventory); public safety (police, fire, emergency management, emergency communications); public utilities (water, sewer, refuse); public works (street maintenance, traffic control, engineering, buildings and grounds, erosion and sediment control, stormwater); parks and recreation (programs, parks maintenance, horticulture, cemeteries); library, economic development and tourism, human resources, planning and GIS, information technology, building code enforcement and zoning administration and enforcement.

It is appropriate that there is no mention of his involvement in securing funding for the WTA because that was never his job. I didn't see him for several years after he resigned. Then I ran into him at an event in the Skyline Drive National Park, and we had a cordial conversation. We've chatted since then. Participating in forcing Walker's resignation was one of the most unpleasant episodes of my time on Council, but in my opinion, it was best for the city.

With July approaching, the first order of business for the new Council was to select a Mayor. Leading up to the organizational meeting, Nancy Dowdy suggested that we make Lorie Smith the Vice Mayor. It would be a show of unity, and besides, Smith had so much experience with the School Board and had attended many of the regional and state meetings. It sounded okay to me, but the rest of the majority felt it would be a slap in the face to those who had voted for us. Strange as it seems, none of us in the majority actually wanted the job. We came to an agreement. Tim Williams would accept a nomination for Mayor with the understanding that I would take it after two years.

At the organizational meeting held on July 1, 2008, Williams was unanimously elected Mayor. Dowdy officially nominated Smith for Vice Mayor and explained her reasoning. In a very uncommon move, Smith seconded the motion to nominate herself, and it died on a 2–3 vote. Allen then nominated me for Vice Mayor, and Williams seconded the motion. It passed on a 3–2 vote without further discussion. Williams, Allen, and I were in favor; Dowdy and Smith opposed. Up until that point, it was the only time during my years on Council that a vote for the Mayor or Vice Mayor was not unanimous.

Chris Graham took losing the election very badly and began to write untrue stories in the *Augusta Free Press*. I was sympathetic, remembering what it felt like to lose an election. And it must have been extra hard to lose one you were expected to win. So, I invited him to lunch. It is so important for capable people to become involved in the political process, and my motivation was to keep him involved. I advised him not to be discouraged and not to burn bridges but to stick with his ambitions.

I also suggested that he make certain that he was writing the truth in his online newspaper. He asked me for an example of a story that was not the truth. He had incorrectly reported that I would be the Mayor. Off the record, I let him in on

It embarrassed and offended Mayor Williams

the decision about Mayor Williams, which was not yet public information. At my request, he held off on printing the decision until it was made public. But then he reported that I had spoken with him off the record and went on to give the details of what I had shared with him.

He had asked why Williams was chosen to be Mayor instead of me. I didn't have a real answer to that, so I unwisely came up with something off the cuff. I said that there hadn't been a Mayor from Ward A for a while, and besides, Williams could probably use the extra money. The Mayor gets $100 more per month than a Councilman. Tim Williams didn't want the job, and he didn't even know it paid $100 more. We never even discussed this issue. I've never figured out why Graham printed my off-the-record comment. It embarrassed and offended Mayor Williams and his wife and made for very hard feelings between us. I apologized profusely to them, but for a few days, Williams wouldn't even speak to me. He gradually seemed to get over it, but I don't think he ever fully trusted me again. I felt horrible because he had been my friend and supporter. I had set out with good intentions, but I blew it. Graham's hostile feelings toward me and the other members of Council grew.

CHAPTER 9

Saving and Spending

On May 5, 2006, during Council's regular business meeting, a hearing was held on the city's capital improvement plan (CIP) for the years 2007–2011. The plan to build a new west end fire station came to my attention for the first time. It had been included in the CIP before I came onto Council.

I noted that the cost of building the new station would be $2.1 million. (Neighboring Staunton had just built one for $1 million.) During this meeting, the operational costs for the new station were discussed. Those costs included salaries for 14 new firemen to staff the new station for a total of about $1 million each year.

I felt that we needed to take another look at the CIP and identify some priorities such as stormwater infrastructure upgrades. We had already saved the city approximately $4 million by moving the Health Department to new quarters rather than building a new facility.

The Fire Chief, Charlie Scott, gave several talks on the subject of a new station and made a presentation at a January 2007 work session. His pitch was that the new station would shorten the time between the fire truck leaving the station and arriving at the fire. And he claimed that having a new station would reduce response times and fire insurance rates for the residents of the city. Neither of those claims is entirely accurate. Insurance rates are related to the International Organization for Standardization classifications which provide an objective, countrywide criterion that aids fire departments in planning and budgeting for facilities, equipment, and training.

The organization collects and analyzes relevant data on municipal fire-protection efforts in communities throughout the United States and assigns each a classification based on a Fire Suppression Rating Schedule. Class 1 represents exemplary public protection, and Class 10 indicates that the area's fire-suppression program doesn't meet the minimum standards. Waynesboro's fire company is rated as a Class 4, and the addition of a new fire station would not change that or lower the residents' insurance rate.

My research showed that it would raise the department's ratings more to make improvements that would increase efficiency. Training as to the layouts of Waynesboro's major buildings (wiring schematics, heat sources, chemical storage locations, etc.) and an upgraded 911 call center with state-of-the-art equipment would raise ratings.

My research also brought to light that Waynesboro didn't have a traffic signal preemption system, which most cities in the area utilize. Traffic lights, equipped with special infrared receiving devices, change when a signal is sent from a special transmitter in an emergency vehicle. A vehicle equipped with a preemption device can use it when approaching a red light to immediately change the signal to green. This clears the intersection of traffic, so the emergency vehicle can get through more rapidly.

I also learned that a new fire station could reduce response time in only 38 percent of the city compared to preemption devices, which would reduce response time across 100 percent of the city. The one-time cost of preemption devices was around $300,000. That's about $2.7 million less than the cost to build the new station and staff it with 14 new firemen for just the first year.

Dowdy justified the need for a new station by citing the response time of a 2:00 a.m. call to a fire in the west end of town. It took 13 minutes to get to the fire from when the call came in to the dispatcher.

Response times are broken into four stages: (1) the time between the call coming to the dispatcher and the message getting to the fire station; (2) the time between the fire station receiving the call and the fire truck leaving the station; (3) the time between the fire truck leaving the station and arriving at the fire; and (4) the time between getting to the scene of the fire and beginning to pump water.

Stage 3 is the only response time that is affected by the distance from the fire station and how long it takes to make the drive. If the call comes in late at night the firemen have to wake up, get dressed, and put on all their gear. This affects stage two and would have been a factor in the 13-minute response time Dowdy cited.

Mayor Reynolds stated that there was no clear consensus regarding a new west end fire station. The discussion dragged on for the next few months as Council members locked in on their respective positions. Including the fire station money, the City Manager wanted to borrow a total of $26 million for capital improvements. This would include money to pay off prior bonds, robbing Peter to pay Paul. Needless to say, Williams and I were against this idea plain and simple. Since it took four of five Council members to approve borrowing money, we were at a stalemate. City staff and some of Council came up with the idea of a referendum so the citizens could vote on the issues. Letting the people decide sounded like a good idea to me.

On August 27, 2007, a motion was made to approve a resolution requesting the court to order a special election regarding the issuance of public improvement bonds in the maximum amount of $13,995,477 to cover these five projects: (1) $1,248,000 for sidewalk and cross walk improvements; (2) $6,207,552 for stormwater infrastructure improvements; (3) $1,248,000 for library improvements; (4) $2,620,800 for West End fire substation; and (5) $2,671,095 for ballfield improvements. I was absent from the meeting, but I supported the resolution which would allow the community to vote on these expenditures. It passed unanimously 4–0.

There was no clear consensus.

Mayor Reynolds and I were invited to address the Round Table, a group of well-respected individuals who met periodically to learn about community matters. Reynolds spoke in favor of building a new fire station, and I spoke against it. During the Q&A segment, Harold Cook, retired plant manager of the local Hershey's plant, stated that we should not have a referendum. It was Council's job as elected officials to make these decisions, and in his opinion, we should not waste taxpayer money on a referendum.

I questioned the validity of his statement. What could be the harm in having the people decide issues of this importance? Cook is a smart man, but I didn't think his argument was sound. As it turned out, he was right. The people most likely to vote in the referendum were those with a vested interest: firemen, their families, people who would profit from the sale of the land and the contractors who would build the station. The general public didn't know the details and related costs, so they were not in a position to make an informed decision.

Only about 70 percent of the people who are eligible to vote are registered, and on the day of the referendum, there was only a 31 percent registered voter turnout. The vote was 1,899 to 1,407 in favor of building the west end fire station. That's more people than usually turn out for a referendum, but this one was packaged with a general election for a few state offices. The math works out to less than 12 percent of the eligible voters making a decision to build a west end fire station.

That's what Cook meant by it being the Council's job. We had all the information needed to make a wise decision, but passed the buck to those who didn't. I was surprised that there were 1,407 who voted against the fire station. Bonds for the sidewalks and the ballfields failed. The stormwater and library improvement bonds passed, along with the bond for the new fire station.

As is the case with every referendum, the result of this vote is non-binding. It still required four out of five votes by Council to approve these projects. Not long after the referendum, it was determined that the vote was not legal because the notices were not advertised in the newspaper according to code. But Council concluded that we would accept the results, because it would cost thousands to have another special election on this matter.

Waynesboro Fire Station

As a result of the vote, on January 28, 2008, during a regular Council meeting, an ordinance authorizing public improvement bonds of $10,076,352 was unanimously approved. The bonds would cover the stormwater and library improvements and the acquisition of land and the design and construction of a new west end fire station.

But the fire station was never built because the make-up of the Council changed within 90 days. Allen won the seat vacated by Mayor Reynolds. In light of the referendum, I had reluctantly shifted to supporting the new station, until the design for it came back to the Council and included a museum that would house an old pumper truck and an expensive kitchen. I withdrew my support. We had recently put $30,000 into renovating the kitchen at the main station. But on many days, the firemen drove the fire truck to local restaurants and let the engine sit there running while they went inside to eat lunch. So Council sent the architects back to the drawing board to revise the plans.

When it came down to the nitty gritty, I stated that I would support building the revised fire station, but I would not support hiring 14 new firemen to staff the station. We had over 40 paid fireman on the payroll already, and I wanted to split the company and place some members at each station. That would save the city a million dollars a year. To support the cost of the annual salaries of 14 more firemen, the property tax rate would have to go up at least six cents per hundred dollars. Staunton had split their fire company, and it worked out well for them.

Without the 14 new hires, the Waynesboro fire department was less interested in the new station. The impetus was gone and the plan slowly died. The money we approved for the fire station was eventually used for previously-approved stormwater projects that were sorely needed. Councilwoman Dowdy, who was in favor of the new fire station, commented that if someone got killed in a fire it would be on our shoulders. What a horrible thing to say. There was a death several years later in a trailer fire, but it was less than a mile from the main station and had nothing to do with distance.

Council eventually approved the purchase of the preemption devices for around $300,000. It was a one-time expense and improved response times throughout the city. It has been ten years since the referendum, and the city's fire department, still operating from one station, unfailingly does an outstanding job for the people of Waynesboro.

In this digital age, with an infinite amount of information at our fingertips, there is a lot of

Waynesboro Public Library

discussion about the value of brick-and-mortar libraries. But while gathering resources for this book, I made numerous trips to the Waynesboro Public Library for things that can't be found on the internet. I view the library as an important educational institution and support it with cash donations.

Back at the November 2007 election, voters chose to fund library improvements. In January 2008, the city issued bonds in the amount of $1.248 million for that purpose. In a work session on September 23, 2009, the Council was told that rather than expanding as planned, the library would just be renovating. The expansion could not be done within the $1.248 million budget. I asked if their renovation plans included building a staircase to connect the first floor with the basement floor. In my mind, that was a most important consideration because as it stood, you had to exit the building and walk around to the other side to enter the basement section of the library. This arrangement was inconvenient at the least and miserable during cold or inclement weather.

Nope. Stairs were not included in the renovation plan. I was dumbstruck. How could you even think of spending $1.248 million for renovations and not connect the two floors with indoor steps? I suggested that maybe Council could come up with some additional money to complete a stairway. The rest of the Council agreed, and we sent the planners back to the drawing board to find out what the increased cost would be. I think the library people were a little surprised that I would suggest something that would require more spending because I had the reputation of being tight fisted with the city's money.

At a regular Council meeting on June 28, 2010, we passed an ordinance giving the library an additional $400,000 out of the city's reserve funds to include construction of a stairway. Every time I go to the library and go up or down those stairs, I take a little pleasure in knowing I had something to do with that practical decision.

Not long after Bruce Allen was elected to Council in 2008, he noticed that the city had a large storage tank of used motor oil that had been drained from the city's vehicles during oil changes. The city has hundreds of vehicles so there's a lot of used oil. Every so often it was picked up by a company that would recycle it.

Allen reasoned that the used oil could fuel a heating system in the city's garage. The city would have to invest in an oil burning furnace but that expense would be recovered within a year or two, and the savings on utility costs would be ongoing. The staff and the rest of Council saw the merit and the oil burning furnace was purchased and installed.

One afternoon later that winter, I accompanied Allen to the city garage to see how the oil furnace was performing. The employees who maintain city vehicles said they were satisfied with the temperature in their shop. It was only in the high 20s outside, but it was fairly comfortable where they were working.

Since we were there, we decided to check out the rest of the city shops. We went into an adjoining garage where the

We sent the planners back to the drawing board

city's big trucks and equipment are stored. A number of large gas heaters were mounted on the ceiling of the expansive space, all burning at full throttle. No one was around and the over-sized garage door to the outside was wide open. We finally located an employee to ask why the door was open, and he casually answered that someone forgot to close it. So much for our efforts to save money.

Before leaving, we stopped by the employee break room where four prison inmates were playing a card game under the watchful eye of an armed guard. The deal was that the prisoners would work for free on city projects such as stormwater infrastructure clean outs, street projcets, etc., but we had to pay the guard's salary of around $57,000 per year. It seemed we weren't getting what we paid for since we were paying the guard to watch the prisoners play cards. We walked back through the garage at around two o'clock and saw that the big door was now closed.

On another occasion, the city's budget director mentioned to me that the electric bill for a little building in the city cemetery was bigger than the electric bill for City Hall. Allen and I decided to take a ride over to the cemetery. We found five or six electric heaters running on high in the sales office. Several ceiling tiles were missing, and you could see daylight through the roof rafters. Not only were we heating the outdoors again, we were doing it with electricity, which is considerably more expensive than gas.

CHAPTER 10

The Election of 2010

In 2010, Nancy Dowdy decided for personal reasons to not seek reelection. Council had been more or less evenly split with Dowdy and Smith on the liberal side, Allen and me on the conservative side, and Mayor Williams breaking the tie votes. Williams generally leaned to our side, but he had voted with Dowdy and Smith against Allen and me to pass a 3.5 percent property tax increase—the most critical vote of the year.

Lorie Smith decided she would run again. She had no competition at first. Her former opponent, Reo Hatfield, was following his business interests to Charlottesville and was engaged to be married in the fall. With the help of some of our supporters and the conservative recruiters, Allen and I began to look in earnest for a qualified candidate to run against her. While searching voter registration lists, I was reminded of a fellow named Mike Harris who had helped me in my campaign two years before. He was a polished speaker who carried himself with confidence. As a retired Virginia State Trooper, Harris had assisted Republican Bob McDonnell with his campaigns for Virginia Attorney General and Governor. (McDonnell held state office from 1992 until 2014 and carries the distinction of being the only Virginia governor to be indicted or convicted of a felony. His conviction was later overturned on appeal.)

Allen and I met with Harris to see if he would be interested in running for Council. He appeared to live by conservative principles that would align with ours rather than with Smith's. He was very receptive to the idea, needed to talk it over with his wife, and said he would get back shortly with a decision. We offered to do everything we could to get his name out into the community if he chose to run.

We visited with him and his wife to answer questions and walk them him through the procedures for running for City Council. He would be running in Smith's ward, Ward D, the west end and more affluent part of the city. To run for Council, you are required to have resided in the Ward for which you run for only <u>one</u> day. And you must be a registered voter. That's it! Those are the only requirements for a job in which you, and four others who have met the identical meager requirements, will set policy for the city and decide on the taxes that the citizens will have to pay. Kind of ironic isn't it? Being a Council member is a very, very important job that in effect requires no qualifications.

The first step is to get 125 registered voters to sign a petition stating your intent to be on the ballot. You can have volunteers get the signatures for you. If that's the case, they must submit a notarized statement to the registrar saying they personally witnessed each signature. The standard practice is to turn in 150 signatures, because some people who aren't registered will sign because they are embarrassed to admit it. In Waynesboro only about 70 percent of the people eligible to vote are registered.

Harris agreed to run and rounded up his signatures. Game on! He hammered Smith on her tax-and-spend history and her continual push for taxpayer money to fund the Wayne Theatre.

As a hometown girl who had served on the School Board for four years and had beaten Hatfield for the Council seat she now held, Smith was a very formidable candidate. But the local newspaper endorsed Harris, who shared their opposition to spending taxpayer money on the Wayne Theatre. (Later the newspaper flip-flopped on the theater issue and has since done it again. Publishers come and go bringing their own perspectives.) The endorsement for Harris read:

> ...we chose Mike Harris over incumbent Lorie Smith. We're still not sure about Harris's zero-based budgeting approach—the current council's record of spending has been one of prudence—but we think his take-charge stance on economic development could be useful....

With Dowdy retiring, Ward C was up for grabs. Life-long resident Jeff Freemen was asked by some friends to run. He was a former Atlantic Coast Conference girls basketball official and was viewed as a polite and conservative man. Then Robert Johnson threw his hat into the ring. He was more liberal than Freeman, and it was thought that Dowdy's supporters had recruited him to follow in her footsteps.

Johnson worked for the highway department and struck me as a very smart and sincere fellow, but he wasn't good at public speaking, which was a drawback. Freeman was retired, which allowed him more time for campaigning. He got the newspaper's endorsement and had many politically conservative activists backing him. I felt that with all these advantages Freeman would win handily. But when Election Day came around, the votes for the Ward C seat totaled 1,530 for Freeman and 1,104 for Johnson. It was a much closer race than I expected.

Ward C was up for grabs.

On the afternoon of Election Day, both Harris and Smith still had volunteers encouraging citizens to get out the vote. For the Ward D seat, Harris beat Smith 1,474 to 1,333. The next day's newspaper read:

> The power shift that began two years ago on the Waynesboro City Council culminated Tuesday with victories by conservative newcomers that swept away the last of the once popular opposing bloc.

The minority faction was gone and Council was seated with five conservative men. Maybe now we could get some stuff done!

Again, the first order of business is to pick the Mayor. Williams said in 2008 that he would take the job if I would take it over in 2010. I had agreed. I didn't really want to be Mayor, but Williams had taken his turn, and now, someone else had to step up. I would have been comfortable with Allen. He had a lot of common sense and would represent the city well. But he had only been on Council for two years and felt he wasn't ready. That left Freeman and Harris, but Allen, Williams, and I couldn't get behind either of them because they'd just been elected, and we really didn't know them yet. It came down to me, and after all, I had told Williams I would take it. He and Allen and I would be making the decision. So, on July 1, 2010, at the organizational meeting, I was unanimously elected Mayor, basically by default, and Allen was elected Vice Mayor. There was no way of knowing how divisive being Mayor would become over the next couple of years.

Smith vowed to stay involved in the community, and Johnson backed out of the political scene entirely. I admire people who step up and run for office. It takes a lot of courage. Most people don't want the public looking into their private lives, and others are afraid of the public humiliation they associate with being defeated. Some people have a generally low opinion of politicians, and that's another thing that gets in the way of recruiting good candidates. Sure, a few have self-serving agendas, but it's unfair for those few to give the whole lot a bad reputation. This negativity harms the city as well as the country because we desperately need qualified, hard-working people to run for office. And by qualified, I mean possessing applicable skills, not simply residing in a particular ward for one day.

ROSANNE WEBER/STAFF

Frank Lucente, left, talks Thursday with Bruce Allen. Lucente was voted the mayor of Waynesboro and Allen was voted vice mayor.

The News Virginian July 2, 2010

Looking forward to 'great things'

Frank Lucente, center, newly elected mayor of Waynesboro, meets Thursday with City Manager Mike Hamp, left, and Assistant City Manager Jim Shaw.

Lucente takes on top job

Leader of conservative bloc appointed mayor   INSIDE
The next step

CHAPTER 11

The Mayor

To be elected Mayor by the Council is to become the formal leader of the Council and the city, an honor for sure. The Mayor is largely a ceremonial position with meetings to run and ribbons to cut. You still only get one vote, and you don't have much more power than the other Council members. The city charter says the Mayor sets and approves the agenda. That gives some control over what is voted on and discussed, but I intended to share the privilege with Council members.

My primary goal was for the city to run more efficiently, which would lower taxes for the citizens. I challenged myself to set an example for other cities to follow. Aspiring to total transparency, I announced my goals and ambitions to the city staff and Council. I don't recall asking any of my fellow Councilmen about their goals; I don't even know if they had any goals. Assuming that we were all on the same page and desired the same outcomes was a big mistake.

A number of Council's functions are advised by local and regional boards and commissions such as the Cultural Commission, Board of Building Code Appeals, Valley Program for the Aging Services Council, and the Historical Commission. The boards and commissions are seated by our citizens, some elected and some appointed. There are a total of 89 seats, 13 of them vacant as of this writing.

In July of 2010, a seat opened up on the Economic Development Authority board. It was up to Council to appoint someone to fill the seat, preferably unanimously. I thought that an attorney, John Hill would be a valuable board member, so I asked him if he would accept the appointment. He agreed. Then I canvased the Council and found that one member was strongly opposed to Hill taking the seat based on some previous experience. I had done things in the wrong order and put myself in an embarrassing spot. I had to go back to Hill and fix it. He was okay with not serving, understanding that someone on Council was opposed.

I began to comprehend what it meant to be in a leadership position. It dawned on me that I had the skill to influence people and sometimes get them to do what I wanted them to do. The weight of the office sank in as I became aware of the possibility of leading in the wrong direction. Think Jim Jones. I was determined to use my leadership skills to help the people of Waynesboro and strengthen our community.

Late in the summer, there were a couple of murders in the east end of Waynesboro with one corpse found in an alley by a large, low-rent, run-down stretch of apartments located on Commerce Avenue. In another case, the murderer resided in one of those apartments. Word around town was that a lot of drugs were being sold there. The murders heightened the city administration's awareness of the conditions around the complex. The building inspector started to do some inspections and crack down on the building code violations.

I was only vaguely aware of the inspections until Bobby Jardeen, the landlord of the apartments called and asked for a face-to-face meeting. He felt he was being unfairly picked on by the city because of the murders. That didn't sound right, but I told him I would check into it.

City Manager Mike Hamp and Assistant City Manager Jim Shaw filled me in on some of the things going on at the Commerce Avenue apartments. They confirmed the drug dealing rumor and said that people were congregating outside the apartments, and that there were numerous code violations in the building. I asked them whether they were coming down extra hard on the property owner or simply enforcing the City Code, and they assured me they were working strictly within the law.

I got back to Jardeen and told him my findings. He was not happy with the answer, but the fact that I had checked into it pacified him. I asked him to let me know if something came up that he felt was not in accordance with the law.

I thought that was the end of it, but a few weeks later, I heard that Councilman Harris was spreading a rumor that I told the City Manager not to enforce the building code at the Commerce apartment complex. Why would I do that? I invited Harris to meet me for lunch at the Moose Club. Without placing blame, I brought up the rumor. I casually mentioned that when you spread a rumor about someone it always gets back to that person. I dealt with it that way because I didn't want to jeopardize our ability to work together.

Then Councilman Allen reported that he had heard the rumor. I scheduled a meeting for Allen, Hamp, Shaw, and me. I asked Hamp to tell Allen what he and I had discussed about the apartments. Hamp confirmed that I had instructed him to enforce the Code, but not go beyond the standards that other landlords were expected to uphold. Allen was satisfied, but this drove a wedge between Harris and me. He lined himself up politically with Freeman as well as Williams at times.

Meth labs were found in two apartments.

In the spring of 2011, Tonya Hardy acquired ownership of the apartment complex on Commerce Avenue in a divorce settlement. She immediately began to make improvements. She opened it up for the city building inspectors and allowed the police to bring in drug sniffing dogs. Meth labs were found in two of the apartments.

Hardy evicted the drug dealers and empowered the other tenants to get involved in cleaning up the public areas. She put a program in place for those who were having trouble paying their rent. She would give a tenant $10 per hour credit toward their rent for every hour of community service they performed. The program is still in effect today. All of the apartments have been remodeled, and no more trouble has come from that particular apartment complex.

I was called to the City Manager's office around the first of August 2011. I was shown a photograph of some graffiti written on the inside wall of a porta-john. I was a little shocked to read the threat on my life:

> To Mayor Frank Lucente
> We live at 231 Port Republic Rd.
> Fuck you. We will kill
> you soon. You cannot
> stop us from selling Meth

I was told that it was found at one of the city parks about seven days ago. I was stunned to be learning about a death threat that had been known about for a week! When I asked about the delay in telling me, I was given the lame excuse that the Chief of Police had been out of town all week. This was rather disconcerting, but I rationalized that it was probably someone trying to get the occupants of 231 Port Republic Road in trouble. If it had been a serious threat, I felt the perpetrators, who were never identified, would not have included their own address.

I hadn't been Mayor long when I wrote these observations in my journal:

1. You can't make everyone happy.
2. There's a lot of ego to work around.
3. You must give others credit.
4. There is a lack of leadership in the community.

I also recorded my thoughts and activities. I had not looked at them for five years and brought them out recently to jar my memories for this book. It is fascinating to go through the material. Much of what I wrote was mundane, such as *took a shower* abbreviated as TAS; *walked the dog* abbreviated as WTD; *read the paper* abbreviated as RTP, etc. But I also recorded the daily business of the city such as the following excerpts:

(August 19) I met with Roger Willets about his desire to sell [the city] the 170 acres of land that he and Charlie Obaugh owned. I told him I was in favor of keeping talks open, but not in favor of buying the land for $4 million with no plan.

(August 20) Bruce Allen gave me a heads up that the rest of Council was upset that I had met with Roger Willets to discuss the city purchase of his land. They were going to address this in a closed session during the regular Council meeting to be held on the 23rd. Someone is stirring the pot and trying to split this Council. I met with Jeff Freemen and explained what I had done and he seemed good with my explanation.

(August 23) During the closed session after the Council meeting, members of the Council criticized me for having a meeting with Roger Willets. Allen saved me by showing that some of the other members of Council [have had conversations in this manner]. The others folded after [Allen] failed to participate in the assault, and the matter died.

(September 15) There was an article in the newspaper about my plan to get the tax rate lowered about 3 percent. This did not go over well with the other Council members. This was a mistake on my part and I should have given [them] a heads up. I called each Council member...and apologized.

(September 16) Went to William Perry to talk to the second graders and had a question and answer period. I remember one little boy asked me if I lived in a log cabin. Another child asked me if I had a gun!...It was one of my best days as Mayor. I had so much fun with those kids.

(September 22) I met with school officials and our City Manager and Assistant City Manager at Westwood Elementary school. The meeting went well, but I was criticized for wearing shorts to the meeting. I felt that these people were nitpicking and not at all concerned about the issues at hand. I feel like I'm beginning to lose effectiveness.

(September 27) Council meeting went well except that Harris indicated he was changing his vote on the ball field concession stand and this made me the swing vote. I postponed the vote until the next Council meeting because I was not prepared to be the swing vote and needed time to gather more facts than had been presented at the meeting.

I was learning through trial and error that when in public office, you have to be mindful of everything you do and say. Talking to the press is especially tricky because your words can be distorted, taken out of context, or simply used against you. Soon you realize that most everyone has an agenda, and the Staunton *News Leader* newspaper is certainly no exception. They take a very liberal view of how government should be run and of the decisions being made on the public's behalf.

One of their new reporters, Calvin Trice, interviewed me on October 2. He asked me what I thought of the fire department, their pay, and their working conditions. I measured my answers carefully to leave my options open during the upcoming budget requests. I started with, "Calvin, this is off the record." Then I acknowledged the heroic measures taken by firemen during the 9/11 World Trade Center event. And I expressed my opinion that some firemen across the country have played on that tragedy to get more benefits and pay.

About two hours after I said goodbye, Trice called me to say his editors were going to print what I said about the firemen. I argued that I had made that comment off the record, but he said he had not agreed to that. Terribly upset, I told him to tell his editors that if they printed my off the record comment, that would be my last interview with them as long as I was on Council.

An hour or so later, Trice called back and said that they had decided to leave the quote out because it was irrelevant in the context of the story.

I had narrowly escaped what could have been a very embarrassing moment in my early days as the Mayor of Waynesboro. And I learned that I shouldn't always speak my mind.

In mid-October, I came up with the idea of removing the city's name from the citizens' bi-monthly water and sewage bill. We had built a new water treatment plant and a new sewage treatment plant and were replacing a lot of old water and sewage pipe. These were expensive upgrades, and we had to increase the rate each household was paying. Many residents complained.

I thought that if the bills weren't associated with the city, if it just looked like a bill from a water company, the complaints might stop. People might accept it the way they accept their other utility bills. I never understood their complaints anyhow.

The city takes a gallon of water from a spring, treats it, and pipes it to your house. You drink it, cook with it, and use it for washing cars and dishes and laundry. You bathe in it and use it to flush away your bodily waste. It all drains neatly out of sight through city pipes to the city sewage treatment plant where it is restored to the condition it was in before you used it. Then it's discharged into the river for the process to begin again. The city measures your usage and sends you a bill. All this for a little over a penny a gallon!

The same people who complain about the price of city water will go into a convenience store and pay more than a $1.25 for a pint of water. But nothing came of my idea to remove the city's name from the water bill.

———————————

Anything for which the city bills its residents is thought by some to be a tax, and taxes are always fuel for a heated discussion. On the one hand, there are those who complain about taxes, on the other hand there are those who push for higher taxes because they have a special interest that could benefit from the city having more money. They may think that increased taxes will result in money for the Wayne Theatre, or they may be a city employee or teacher who will see a pay raise as a result. A family with three children in school may see an increase in the school budget as a benefit that outweighs the cost of the higher taxes.

Alexander Fraser Tytler (October 15, 1747– January 5, 1813) was a Scottish advocate, judge, writer, and Professor of Universal History. In his lectures, he expressed a critical view of democracy in general and spoke specifically to those with self-serving attitudes toward taxation:

> A democracy is always temporary in nature; it simply cannot exist as a permanent form of government. A democracy will continue to exist up until the time that voters discover that they can vote themselves generous gifts from the public treasury. From that moment on, the majority always votes for the candidates who promise the most benefits from the public treasury, with the result that every democracy will finally collapse due to loose fiscal policy, which is always followed by a dictatorship.

We're moving in that direction on the national level, and would be in Waynesboro if not for safeguards against over-spending. That doesn't keep special interest groups from trying though. By Code, the city can only borrow so much money based on its property value, but there is no limit on raising taxes. In 2010, our tax rate was the seventh lowest of 39 cities in Virginia. Many thought that was too low, but I wanted to achieve the very lowest tax rate while still maintaining the best schools and services. My critics thought that was impossible, which brings me back to my primary goal of running the city more efficiently.

There are many ways in which efficiency can save the tax payers money if we simply pay attention. The SPCA was charging Waynesboro, Staunton, and Augusta County excessive fees when our animal control officer delivered stray or lost cats and dogs to them. In early December, we set the wheels in motion to establish the Shenandoah Valley Animal Services Center, which meets our needs and saves all three municipalities a considerable amount of money.

In general, most people aren't aware of whether or not the government runs efficiently. The best place to find efficiency is in the business sector where management is driven to achieve maximum productivity with minimum wasted effort or expense, both essential to competing and profit making.

In government, where there is no opportunity for profit per se, the incentive for conducting business competitively or efficiently is less obvious. In Waynesboro, there is little or no competition for education, infrastructure, water and sewer, etc. The more inefficient the government becomes, the more money is needed from the taxpayers.

The Post Office loses money every year but gets money from the taxpayers' treasury to stay operational, in spite of the loss. There's no way that Federal Express or UPS would survive if they lost money. In fact, those two companies exist because of the inefficiency of the US Postal Service.

On December 9, 2010, the topic of giving city employees an extra paid day off for Christmas came up right on schedule. Every year, a couple of weeks before Christmas, the City Manager would ask Council to give the employees Christmas Eve off as a thank you for all their hard work. And, at that time of year, it is hard to say no because everyone is in the spirit of

I was accused of being a Scrooge

giving. I was accused of being a Scrooge because I was against giving the extra day off.

The average number of paid holidays per year for employees in the private sector is around seven days, and the city already has ten paid holidays. Being asked to make this decision right before Christmas made me feel emotionally blackmailed.

Not all employees could even take that day off. The firemen, policemen, sewage plant workers, water plant workers, and other essential employees still have to work on holidays. When non-essential employees take a holiday, these essential employees have to be paid overtime. That's about a $60,000 additional expense per day to the city. It was the taxpayers who would be paying for the generosity, and a lot of them have to work at their jobs on Christmas Eve.

In addition, the City Manager asked for Christmas bonuses for the employees. I had asked him repeatedly to include these requests at budget time, not right before the holiday when denying the request made us look bad. But he never put the holiday considerations in the budget. I suspect he knew that Council would not approve the eleventh holiday or the bonuses during the January budget season when we were always looking for savings, not added costs.

After much discussion among Councilmen about the additional holiday and bonus for 2010, both were defeated on a 5–0 vote that year. Since then, there have been a number of times when the holiday was extended. For example, in 2012 Christmas fell on a Tuesday so the non-essential employees were given Christmas Eve off to allow a four-day holiday weekend. And in 2014, Christmas fell on a Thursday, so they were also given Friday off to make a four-day holiday weekend, etc.

On April 4, 2011, the City Manager presented his 2012 budget. It included raising the lodging tax from five percent to six percent, the meals tax from five percent to six percent, and the cigarette tax from 20 cents a pack to 24 cents a pack.

Those in governmental bureaucracies ask for more money than they actually need. The staff knows that it is Council's job to look for ways to improve efficiency and that means budget cuts. The property tax was 70 cents per $100 of assessed value and the City Manager was requesting that we raise that to 78 cents per $100. Every two years, the individual properties in the city are reassessed and a new value is determined. Because the prices of homes had gone down during the recession, property values went down proportionally in the assessment. In order for the city to collect the same amount of money as the year before, we would have to raise the property tax rate to the requested 78 cents per $100. This practice is called equalizing, and basically, the property owner would pay about the same amount of real estate tax as before. Higher property value taxed at a lower rate is about the same as lower property value taxed at a higher rate.

After the budget presentation, all of the Councilmen were in favor of equalizing the real estate tax rate and raising the lodging tax on hotel rooms. Neither of those measures would have much impact on what Waynesboro's residents routinely spend. Almost all of the lodging taxes are paid by travelers passing through from the interstate.

However, we were not all in favor of raising the meals tax, and no one was in favor of raising the cigarette tax. We had learned the hard way that our revenue from cigarette tax actually dropped when we raised the rate before. People went to a little convenience store right outside the city limits to get their smokes.

I am not sure how much of the meals taxes are paid by people who reside outside of the city, but it is a significant amount. Of course, Waynesboro residents also eat in local restaurants, but unlike real estate taxes, this is a discretionary expenditure.

Then we realized that a combined lodging tax and meals tax increase could offset the real estate tax by three cents per $100. So, Councilmen Allen, Williams, and I decided that we only needed to raise the property tax to 75 cents per $100, which would actually lower property taxes for the residents.

It was a little tough for me to vote to raise meals taxes because I have vested interests in a local eatery, but I felt it was best for our citizens to get the property tax break, so I went along with the other Councilmen and voted in favor.

At the regular Council meeting on May 9, Freeman introduced a 78 cent per $100 property tax rate and Allen introduced a 75 cent per $100 rate. On May 23, 2011, Freeman moved and Harris seconded a motion to adopt the 78-cent rate. It failed on a 2–3 vote with Williams, Allen, and me opposed. Then Allen moved and Williams seconded a motion for the 75-cent rate, and it passed 3–2.

This was the last major act of our first year as the new five-man Council. It was the first time we had lowered property taxes in a long time, and two of the five conservative Councilmen had voted against it.

CHAPTER 12

The Trip to China

I came to Waynesboro in 1990. One of the first things I noticed after opening my business in downtown was a number of Chinese businessmen walking about the streets with cameras, snapping pictures of everything. Their interest, I was told, was in the DuPont plant with its 1,500 employees. They wanted to learn how the plant made nylon and Lycra.

Fast forward to 2008. Tom Reider, a member of the Waynesboro Economic Development Authority (EDA) who had replaced me on the Housing Authority Board when I was appointed to Council, visited China to tour some industries. He was part of a delegation that included Tom Sikes, the General Manager of REO Distribution Services, and Eddy Shek, a native of China now living in Charlottesville. Shek is an intermediary and facilitator who explores opportunities for increased trade between China and Virginia. He made all of the arrangements for this visit. The delegation received an extravagant welcome by officials of the Chinese government.

In exchange, Chinese representatives from the district of Wanzhou in the Chongqing municipality of China were invited to tour our region. They visited the Hershey plant, the Blue Ridge Parkway, and the Mish brothers farming operation. The highlight for them was the farm. They could not believe it was privately owned by an individual and were quite curious about its value and the high-tech farming equipment. Sharon Plemmons, a local business woman, made dinner for them in her home. The managers of REO Distribution Services went out of their way to provide a welcome comparable to what Waynesboro's delegation had received during their visit to Wanzhou. According to Eddy Shek, the Chinese people were enchanted by our spacious mountains, the valley lifestyle, and our clean air.

Eddy Shek, Reider, and Sikes collaborated with officials of the Chinese government to establish Waynesboro as a sister city to Wanzhou. It's a city of 1,750,000 with an urban population of 830,000. Waynesboro has a population of only 22,000, but we have industrial interests in common.

For one thing, REO ships goods internationally from its location in Solutions Place, an area in

Waynesboro that had acquired a designation as a Free Trade Zone through the Virginia Port Authority. Wikipedia describes a Free Trade Zone as "...a geographic area where goods may be landed, stored, handled, manufactured, or reconfigured, and re-exported under specific customs regulations and generally not subject to customs duty." This designation lends our industries flexibility in the import business and is meant to create jobs and build our local economy. The Chinese are interested in doing business with industries in Free Trade Zones for the obvious reasons.

In 2011, I received an invitation to join the delegation on their next trip to China for an enormous garden and trade expo in Chongqing and a visit to our sister city. This was an unforeseen benefit of being the Mayor. The entire trip was arranged by the Waynesboro EDA and REO Distribution.

We got our vaccinations and boarded our first flight on November 17, 2011. The traveling party led by Tom Sikes of REO Distribution consisted of: Vice-Mayor Allen and his wife Debbie; Eddy Shek, our go-between, scheduler, and translator; Anne Seaton, employee of REO Distribution; Linda Hershey, president of the Chamber of Commerce; Councilman Mike Harris; my wife, Betty, and me.

Betty and I were provided coach tickets by the Chinese government, but she encouraged me to upgrade to business class. That expense came out of our pockets, but after 14 hours in the air, I was glad to have agreed to the added cost.

First, we flew from Charlottesville to Washington DC and then over the Arctic Circle to arrive in Beijing 14 hours later. From Beijing, we had a three-hour flight to Chongqing. We got to our hotel by 10 p.m. on November 18 and hit the sack immediately. It was the hotel's practice to reduce the power in the middle of the night to save energy, so our room became stuffy, and our sleep was restless. We were up for a Chinese-American breakfast at 7:30 a.m. Then our group boarded a 16-passenger van for China's 8th International Expo.

When we arrived at the Expo, I was separated from the rest of my group and escorted like royalty to a seating area for dignitaries. Other US cities that were represented included major port cities such as San Francisco, Houston, and Seattle. The Mayor of Waterloo, Canada, sat next to me during the opening ceremony. She was the only representative from Canada there. I was really feeling out of place when my Canadian counterpart asked what I was doing there. I replied that I had no idea, but there I was.

Hundreds of talented Chinese performed for us in ornate fish and dragon costumes. A dramatic ribbon cutting ceremony included festive lanterns, music and dancing, special colorful smoke effects, and fireworks displays.

We toured the Expo, which featured numerous elaborate exhibits. The Chinese government had built and paid for one that represented Waynesboro and Virginia in a lush garden scene of flowers, trees, and walking paths. It highlighted Thomas Jefferson-style architecture, impressive with its rotunda and arches, and a glass house. Eddy Shek told us that for some reason, the people of China love Thomas Jefferson.

Later in the morning, we took our van to a beautiful hotel for lunch. On the way into Chongqing, a city of eight million people, all of the traffic was stopped by police at every intersection to allow us passage to our destination without interruption. We were escorted in front and behind by big black SUVs with blue lights flashing from the grill. This must be the way the President of the United States feels as he passes through our large cities.

Before we ate lunch, the Mayor of Chongqing gave what I can only assume were welcoming remarks since there was no translator. I was one of dozens of honored guests from all over the world, some in interesting native dress. After lunch, we proceeded to a conference where there were a variety of industry workshops and seminars, with only one in English. Mostly, I remember our Chinese hosts proposing that we build a Hershey plant in China like the one we have in Stuarts Draft. They were willing to give us land and funding. I just kept suggesting that they build a plant in Virginia, and let us export the goods to them.

Dinner that first evening was an extravagant international buffet. We were entertained by a variety of performers wearing more spectacular costumes. When we returned to our resident hotel, Allen and I stopped by the bar for a drink to wind down from the day of pageantry. Each of the next four days was similarly exotic.

In Wanzhou, we were shown through an enormous Lycra plant. I kept flashing back to 1990, when I'd witnessed the Chinese men photographing our town. All I could think was that this was Waynesboro's Lycra plant.

Eddy Shek says that after Nixon opened relations between the United States and China back in the 70s, the first thing Ding Xiaoping (chairman of the Communist Party) did was to send all the Chinese children of high government officials to schools in the US. Once the students completed their educations, they returned to China steeped in the virtues of capitalism. They were not reverting to the old ways of their homeland, and many are now in leadership positions.

Another draw toward capitalism occurred after the fall of the Berlin Wall in 1989. The Chinese government was able to compare the oppressive communist East German economy and the progressive capitalist West German economy. So, they made some adjustments in their system to develop capitalist enterprise zones. Within the

Signing Wanzhou and Waynesboro sister city agreement.

zones, citizens can own property and businesses and live under a capitalistic system maintained under communist rule.

We had plenty of free time to explore the region and do some shopping. We shared a good laugh when my wife came out of a store and earnestly commented that everything in there looked like it was made in China. I'll share some of the most interesting things I observed about this ancient and distinctively different culture.

All capable Chinese people go to school for six years. After that, they are evaluated and some continue with school and some do not, based on ability and achievement. The ones who don't continue are given jobs in labor fields such as street sweeper, trash collector, factory workers, etc. The ones that go on with school are evaluated again at the 12-year mark. Some are sent to learn and work in trades such as carpentry, drafting, and welding. The best students go on to college, and when they finish, they are assigned to professions in sciences, education, etc. That's why their students' standardized test scores seem so high in contrast to US students. Only a select group of the best students take the tests in China, unlike the US where all students take the tests in our no-child-left-behind education system.

Every able-bodied person works and the work is non-stop. I filmed construction underway on both sides of our moving vehicle continuously for 20 minutes on Sunday afternoon between 4:00 and 4:30 p.m. They have overbuilt their cities, creating an excessive inventory of unoccupied malls and housing.

Most all the land is utilized for something. I observed vegetable gardens being tended on the sides of the four-lane highways, where it would not be allowed in the US. I've learned that their rivers were polluted, yet they appear to be very clean. I saw workers in a small barge collecting sticks and debris from the water for some future usage or disposal.

The work is non-stop.

They use Western medications as well as many natural and holistic Eastern remedies. The air pollution is so bad that I didn't see the sun once during my five days there. On some of the streets, I saw individuals who were burning wire they had harvested from junked computers, a process that emits a toxic black smoke.

Chinese people don't waste anything that can be eaten; the vast diversity of foods includes every part of every possible animal or plant. The numeral four is a bad omen because it is pronounced the same as their word for death (shi). The numeral eight is a favorite because it is close to their word for good fortune and prosperity. A license plate number with an eight in it is highly-prized and expensive.

The people are friendly and curious about Americans and many of them seem to truly admire the United States. There are only a thousand or so members of the ruling communist party in the whole country. The rest have no political affiliation but live under communist rule.

This amazing once-in-a-lifetime experience was something only afforded me because of my public service as a member of City Council and Mayor. I am grateful. But I feel that our delegation was exploited a little by the media there. Throughout the trip, I was photographed and interviewed by the newspapers and TV stations. I understand that I appeared on TV news quite often. I think our visit was arranged by the Chinese government to show their people how well their government is doing.

In spite of the touring and interactions, not much in the way of trade happened between Waynesboro and China during the ensuing six years. Councilman Harris had stayed behind to visit an employer who he said might want to build motor bikes in the US, but nothing came of that pursuit. China is busy building industries of their own modeled on the ones we have in the US.

As I write this in 2018, Waynesboro is still a sister city with Wanzhou. Our old DuPont plant, more recently called Invista and owned by Koch Industries, is just a shadow of its former self with 1,200 fewer employees working on very close margins. The decline has been so gradual that the community doesn't even seem to notice. This year, 2018, the plant was sold to a Chinese company. I expect that within a year the whole operation will close and the remaining equipment will be scrapped or shipped to China for use in their factories. More than 50,000 industrial plants in the US have met a similar fate in the last 30 years.

CHAPTER 13

The School Board

In 1993, the citizens of Waynesboro voted to have School Board members elected rather than appointed by City Council. When the board members are appointed, there's always the risk of nepotism and friends or favors influencing the decisions. I remember being very supportive of this initiative at the time because it gave more power to the people. From 1994 until 2016, which was the last School Board election before this book was printed, there were a total of 30 individual school board seats up for election, each holding a four-year term.

In the elections held between 1994 and 2004, five out of fifteen seats were contested races. Between 2006 and 2016, only two out of fifteen seats were contested races. Those two carried one incumbent each, who with the full backing of the other School Board members won the races handily. The pattern of diminishing candidates—typical in elections for many offices these days—results for all practical purposes in self-appointed School Board members.

Does this lack of competition indicate that the School Board is as competent as a School Board needs to be with no room for improvement? Certainly not. I hear complaints all the time about what the schools should or should not be doing for the students of Waynesboro. The schools are not providing a good education, the schools need more resources, people will not move here because our schools are deficient. Due to poor student performance on standardized testing, forty percent of Waynesboro's schools are not even accredited. The students are not to blame.

A number of political analysts support the premise that elected officials who run unopposed are less active in their elected roles than those who are selected through a competitive process. Case in point: 23 out of 30 uncontested School Board races result in unapposed board members who to a great extent are charting the course for a substandard education system for Waynesboro's children.

Often people feel that throwing money at a problem will solve everything. As I write this book, Waynesboro is planning to put $60–80 million more into renovating school buildings. There are many contradictory views nationwide about the quality of school facilities in relation to students' academic performance. According to records from the March 26, 2018, City Council meeting, Mayor Allen stated that he supports renovations that will improve school facilities, but he asked if the high school renovation would guarantee better grades for the students. The superintendent of schools clarified that capital improvements may not have a significant impact on student achievement. But, he said, improving the high school would improve the overall image of the city to residents and prospective residents and may increase enrollment.

Spending money has not proven to advance performance in our relatively new Kate Collins Middle School. The school's SOL test scores (shown on next page) have generally declined, and at this time, the school is not accredited by the Virginia Department of Education. Our residents, School Board, school administration, teachers, and City Council must all work together to develop and implement a comprehensive education improvement plan, and I don't see that happening.

If I had the choice, I would go back to letting the Council appoint the School Board. At least they would choose people more in line with their philosophies, and new energy would come on board with the rhythm of the changing Councils.

KATE COLLINS MIDDLE SCHOOL
SOL TEST RESULTS

	English	Math	History	Science
2004–2005	71	89	88	84
2005–2006	71	58*	76	79
2006–2007	75	66	60*	77
2007–2008	78	78	74	81
2008–2009	82	78	79	88
2009–2010	86	77	80	90
2010–2011	80	75	79	90
2011–2012	84	65*	78	85
2012–2013	65*	67	77	80
2013–2014	64	69	76	66*
2014–2015	66	73	78	73
2015–2016	64	71	81	68
2016–2017	67	76	72*	69
2017–2018	72	81	76	61

New Tests with Increased Rigor and Technology Enhanced Items Implemented

Data from the Virginia Department of Education Accreditation Reports, 2017–2018 results are projections and have not been officially released by DOE, June 21, 2018

I was a member of the committee to remodel the Kate Collins Middle School up until I was appointed to Council. The initial cost was to be $17 million. But before the completion date, the cost had sky rocketed to $23 million. Because I was no longer involved in the project, I never really knew why the costs escalated. The School Board volunteered to help repay some of the debt service for the upgrades with the lottery funds they were allocated by the state each year.

Establishing the city's budget includes determining how much money the city is going to contribute to the School Board to cover the school

Kate Collins Middle School

system's operations. The schools get some money from the state and federal governments, and about a third of their funding comes from the city. The school system is the city's largest single expense.

It was entirely up to Council to decide how much city money the schools got each year. They rely on the City Manager to recommend the dollar amount, which gives him a lot of control over the schools. Doug Walker, the City Manager in the early days of my service, waited until he saw what the federal and state governments were ponying up before determining what the city would contribute. Figuring out the city's contribution was complicated by the fact that the school's budget deadline often fell prior to notice of the state's financial commitment. This situation stirred up a conflict between elected members of the School Board and elected members of City Council every year.

I was chatting with my friend Dave Wolfe about this unhealthy in-fighting, and he suggested we simply give the School Board a percentage of our budget instead. He had seen this done before in another locality. Great idea! It's so beneficial to hear the fresh ideas of qualified citizens when it comes to decision-making.

I presented the concept to Council and the School Board, and everyone responded with enthusiasm because it solved a lot of problems. By basing the percentage on the previous year's city budget the schools would know by December how much money they could expect for their upcoming fiscal year, which would start on July 1. And Walker would know in advance what we would be giving the schools, so it simplified calculating the city budget.

Now, we had to decide what percentage of our budget we were going to contribute to the schools. When Council holds public meetings, we are always required to notify the press. So, we set up a two-on-two meeting because that is not considered a public meeting, and we would not have to complicate things by inviting the press. Tom Reynolds and I represented Council, and Doug Norcross and Cathy Manavel represented the School Board.

We discussed using a 10-year history of the city's discretionary budget to determine what percent of it generally went to the schools. Then we averaged those percentages, and it came out to 41 percent. To seal the deal with the School Board, we offered 42 percent, and they accepted that number. The plan was taken back to our respective bodies and passed unanimously by Council and the School Board. This was in 2007, and it is still in effect to this day.

City Council established a practice of returning all unspent money in the school budget back to the schools for use the following year. This practice kept the schools from spending what they had left over just to be spending it. Not having to worry about forfeiting the surplus was a good incentive for the School Board to be frugal.

This worked really well for years leading up to spring of 2011 when the School Board had a $314,000 surplus from the previous year's budget. In the past, the School Board's debt service for renovations to Kate Collins had been covered by an annual allotment of $200,000 from the state lottery, but the state was no longer distributing those funds. The City Manager proposed that the city retain $177,180 of the $314,000 surplus to help pay the school's portion of the debt. The difference of approximately $137,000 would be returned to the schools for their next budget year. The School Board argued that under the circumstances, they should not have to pay the debt service at all since they had volunteered only their lottery funds in the first place.

When Councilman Freeman, a former teacher, and Councilmen Tim Williams and Mike Harris learned about the City Manager's offer, they began to complain about how the School Board spent its money. They'd been informed that the school superintendent was getting an $8,000+ pay increase, while at the same time, they were cutting back on the number of teachers.

It is up to the School Board to decide how to spend its money. It is not Council's business. Many people, including Councilmen, don't seem to understand that principle, which is clearly established in the City Code.

Freeman, Williams, and Harris thought the city should keep the whole $314,000 surplus to pay down school debt. As far as they were concerned, it was a take-it-or-leave-it deal. If the School Board did not accept the offer to pay

The schools needed every dollar.

$177,180, they would be out all of the $314,000.

I didn't agree that we should keep all of the money, because I knew the schools needed every dollar they could get. I hoped that cooler heads would prevail because, after all, the school had been committed to a payment for debt service in the fiscal 2010 year.

But the three Councilmen complained that they had not seen a full school budget, and they thought that the School Board was less than forthcoming with information about where they were spending the city's money. In contrast, I supported the principle established in the code, recognizing that the School Board was duly elected by the voters, and it was not Council's job to monitor how they spent their money.

As I expected, the School Board rejected the City Manager's offer. So, on May 23, 2011, following a lot of discussion, Freeman moved to apply the entire $314,000 to the school debt. It was seconded by Williams. The vote on the amendment passed 3–2. Bruce Allen and I were opposed. Later, the School Board reconsidered and tried to accept the offer, but it was too late. The deal was off the table, and the entire $314,000 surplus went toward the debt service.

It was rare for Freeman to vote against a city staff recommendation. I have never understood what motivated the majority of the Council to renege on the arrangement to return the year-end surplus. I thought it was a spiteful vote, perhaps something unrelated to the actual issue, and it certainly did not help the Council/School Board relationship. But to date, this is the only exception that has been made to the reasonable practice of giving back the unspent moneys from the previous year's budget.

CHAPTER 14

Chicopee and Opportunity Park

During a regular Council meeting held on April 26, 2010, after a Public Hearing in which none of the general population spoke, the city conveyed approximately seven acres of land to The Polymer Group, Inc. (PGI) by way of the Economic Development Authority (EDA). The company, whose corporate offices are located in Raleigh, North Carolina, was to use this land to expand their Waynesboro Chicopee plant, which manufactures non-woven and laminate materials used in the production of disposable diapers. PGI then began to heavily lobby the city as well as the Commonwealth of Virginia for additional incentives to convince PGI to locate its $65 million expansion at its Waynesboro manufacturing facility.

Industries play localities against each other when it comes to positioning their operations, always looking for the best offers. In this case, Mooresville,

North Carolina, was also vying for PGI's business. Significant tax dollars and 41 new full-time jobs paying average annual wages of $37,939 were at stake.

Waynesboro's City Council and staff were both highly motivated to bring these industrial jobs to Waynesboro, and the Virginia Economic Development Partnership and the Shenandoah Valley Partnership were highly motivated to help secure the project for a Virginia city. The collaborative Economic Incentive Package presented to PGI included: a $750,000 grant from the Governor's Opportunity Fund; a $750,000 performance-based grant from the Virginia Investment Partnership Program; 15 acres of land and a $550,000 site improvement grant from the City of Waynesboro; a six-year estimated $1.75 million real estate and property tax rebate program granted by the city; and a freeze on water and sewer rates for two years granted by the city.

The negotiations were difficult. The more we offered the more they asked for. We bent over backwards and finally came up with the right package. PGI chose the Waynesboro facility over its Mooresville plant. The performance agreement between Chicopee and the city was dated July 21, 2010. Of course, the money from the state agencies helped a lot, but I believe the 15 acres was the thing that put us on top.

In 2010, Mr. Roger Willets, a local attorney and business man, proposed the idea of the city purchasing a 170-acre piece of well-situated land that he and his business partner owned. He called it Opportunity Park. This property was just off the second of three I-64 exits into Waynesboro, had easy access to I-81 and had rail lines running through it. The big disadvantage was that the land was undeveloped and had no infrastructure.

He presented the idea as an industrial park, a place where small and large manufacturing plants could locate. He said it would provide the Economic Development Authority (EDA) with a lure to draw in potential employers. He suggested that there were state grants to help with the cost of developing the park. City staff quickly jumped on board and promoted the idea to City Council.

It was not lost on Council that Willets and his partner Charlie Obaugh, owner of several automobile dealerships in the area, had outbid the city to buy the land at auction in 2001 for about $1 million. Now they wanted to sell it to the city for

$4.2 million and the cost to develop the land would run another $8–11 million. They set the purchase price based on a professional appraisal contracted by the city staff. Buying land requires approval by a super-majority (four out of five Council members must vote in favor), and at the time of Willets' proposal, there was not enough support on Council to move forward with the purchase.

The land was assessed at $3.7 million for tax purposes, meaning that the owners pay taxes based on that value each year. Research showed a half-dozen vacant industrial parks across the state that had sewer and water in place, as well as a dozen or more vacant ones that didn't have infrastructure in place. Some of them were forced to repay state grants that had been contingent on the park being occupied within a certain timeframe.

The jobs climate was then and continues to be mostly out-sourced to manufacturing plants in other countries. I was opposed to purchasing the land and also opposed to spending the $8–11 million for infrastructure on the speculation that some industry might someday be interested in the site.

But the staff was persistent because they felt the land would lure businesses to Waynesboro. I was invited to attend a meeting on April 14, 2011, in my friend Dave Wolfe's office. Wolfe owned a highly successful machine shop that made replacement parts for manufacturers all over the world. He and I had spent many hours over the years talking about actions that might improve the city. He's the one who made the productive suggestion about determining the city's contribution to the school budget. Willets was there as well as Tom Reider. Reider had replaced me when I stepped down from the Housing Authority Board

Three men aimed to convince me.

back in 2005. He now served on the EDA. The three men aimed to convince me that the land purchase would be good for the city. I stood my ground for the reasons I've mentioned, and the conversation went nowhere.

I was urged to meet with Willets a few days later to give him some advice on compromises that might bring Council around. So, I met with him on April 20, 2011, with the understanding that I couldn't speak for Council, I could only speak for myself. Willets had attached a number of inducements to the sale such as a dependency on state grants, delayed land transfer, delayed payment plan, his personal participation in the marketing, etc. I suggested he offer it to the city as a simple purchase, with no inducements, for less than the tax accessed value. I got the sense that he needed to sell the land because of financial difficulties, and that was later confirmed by an associate in the banking business.

Willets asked me to suggest a price. I said maybe $3.5 million. You'll recall it was appraised for $3.7 million. If the city could purchase the land straight out at a more than fair price and didn't have to put up the money for the infrastructure, I would support the purchase.

At that price, I recognized it as a sound investment for the city, a savings account so to speak. By law, the city can't buy stocks or bonds or even gold for that matter, but the city can invest in land with a super-majority vote. This would give the EDA director something to market as is, and at some point down the road the city would benefit greatly. I remained very upfront about my opposition to paying for infrastructure.

So before long, Willets made a proposal to sell the land to the city for $3.6 million. In a closed session on June 13, 2011, following much arm-twisting by the city staff and members of the EDA, Council approved the purchase, and it was just a matter of price now. We made the decision to offer $3.4 million and allow the staff to negotiate up to $3.5 if necessary. Early into the negotiation, our eager staff caved and returned with a counter of $3.55 million. Councilmen Williams, Harris, and Freemen were good with that number, but Allen and I were not. Our reaction was to declare that the $3.5 million offer was no longer on the table.

This move was not unprecedented in this Council's history. Not long ago, Williams, Harris, and Freemen had made the school system a take-it-or-leave-it offer on the return of the year-end funding for the schools. My firm stand on the price of Opportunity Park was a chance to save the city some money and to show the three Councilmen what it's like to be constrained by a take-it-or-leave-it situation.

We knew how badly they wanted to buy the land. New negotiations started. We told the staff that we would now pay no more than $3.4 million for the land. When Willets heard of the new offer, he was very upset and said he would take the previous offer of $3.5, but we told him the $3.5 offer was no longer on the table. He began to lobby us individually, first Allen who did not budge and then me on June 17. Willets kept hounding us, and eventually, we agreed at $3.475 million.

On July 25, 2011, a resolution was passed by the Council to authorize the City Manager to execute an agreement between the city and Waynesboro Opportunity Park, LLC for the acquisition of approximately 170 acres of land located along South Delphin Avenue. I read the following statement, which summarized my opinion of this purchase:

We must create wealth as a nation and as a community if we are to prosper in today's world. This land represents a tool for our community to do just that, by getting in the game. This will allow us the opportunity to compete for these wealth-producing jobs. I've been assured by the City Manager that we can buy this land without raising taxes; that is important to me. The staff supports this deal very strongly. This is the entire staff from the City Manager, Assistant City Manager, the Planners, and also the Economic Development Director. Staff also feels they have the people and the expertise to make something good happen with this project. I always like to look at things in the worst-case scenario. The worst-case scenario is we don't get any takers on the land. If that happens the city does not get hurt on the deal, as inflation in my opinion will continue, and at some point down the road we will make a whole lot on this land. This is a tangible investment. If we are successful in grabbing these wealth-producing jobs, and I feel we have a good chance of doing so, then the community has hit a home run. As a result, I am in favor of purchasing this land. I also feel that Council and staff have done their best in putting this deal together in the best interest of the community.

Councilman Williams was in agreement with my statement saying he had received many calls questioning our decision. He reassured everyone that this land had been a topic of discussion for the seven-plus years he had been on Council. This was not a hasty decision.

The following Resolution was adopted:

Be it resolved by the Council of the City of Waynesboro, Virginia, that the City Manager is authorized to execute an agreement between the City, Waynesboro Opportunity LLC, and Waynesboro Opportunity Park, LLC or their successors in interest, which is related to the acquisition of approximately 170 acres located along South Delphine Avenue.

This motion was passed with affirmative votes from all Council members. The story ran in the Waynesboro paper on July 8.

On July 9, the Staunton *News Leader*, the neighboring town's paper, printed an editorial criticizing me for my support of the purchase because I had received campaign contributions from Willets and Arthur Harrison, the real estate agent for the Willets and Obaugh property.

According to public record, each of those men made a campaign contribution of $600. Believe me when I say that no campaign contribution has ever had any influence on any decisions I've made as a Councilman. Whenever people gave me a contribution I said the same thing. You know what this gets you, don't you? Good government, period!

A controversy ensued. At the July 11 Council meeting, to allow time for public input, I pushed for and got a two-week tabling of the vote to authorize the purchase of the land. Willets was in a rush to complete the deal, but up until now all the talk about Opportunity Park had been carried out in private or in closed Council sessions. Allen and I didn't think it was fair that the taxpayers had not had a chance to weigh in on an action of this magnitude.

There was heated discussion for and against the purchase in the weeks leading up to the Public Hearing. The Wayne Theatre people thought it might diminish their chances for city funding. The public had its chance to weigh in, but only two people showed up at the hearing to make statements. For the most part, Waynesboro's citizens didn't bother to learn the facts and they chose not to take part in the process of deciding on Opportunity Park.

During the July 25, 2011, regular session of City Council, we unanimously approved the purchase of the land. In a public hearing on September 26, a resolution was passed that authorized the city to obtain a tax-exempt bank qualified

There was heated discussion.

loan in an amount not to exceed $3.75 million to purchase Opportunity Park and pay fees associated with the loan.

It wasn't long before the city discovered some obstacles. Opportunity Park did not have a clear title, and some homes on adjoining properties had water rights to use a spring located on the land. By working with the property owners, it was agreed that they would be connected to the city water line at no charge when it came time to bring city water to the site. Until then, they could continue using the spring if they wished. We finally closed the deal in a regular Council meeting on January 23, 2012.

The approximately $30,000 in property taxes per year paid by the previous owners was lost to the city and will be lost every year until the land is put back into private hands. I don't know if our fellow Councilmen got the point Allen and I were trying to make with the take-it-or-leave-it offer, but at least we saved the taxpayers $25,000 on the deal. The city's payment for the land is $25,954.18 per month for 179 months. Not a large sum in a $49 million budget.

Willets was not happy with the outcome. He did everything he could to keep me from being re-elected in the 2012. It seems I had upset the people who didn't want us to buy the land, as well as the people who wanted us to buy it and pay the $8–11 million for the infrastructure. In addition, I aggravated the people who were unhappy that Willets and Obaugh each made a million on the sale (according to public records). It's hard to anger both sides of an issue, but I managed to do it with Opportunity Park.

So far, six years later, nothing has come of the land. Recently a grant has been obtained that will fund the construction of a road through the property. I feel that something good will come out of this eventually. It's a long-term investment, and the city is building equity in a tangible asset.

CHAPTER 15

The Election of 2012

I was undecided about running for a third term. The previous two years had been very disappointing. I had hoped that as a conservative Council, we would have common goals toward a more efficient government that would result in lower taxes and a business-friendly environment. We made some progress, but not nearly as smoothly as I had hoped.

I wanted to make my decision early, so that if I chose not to run, others would have plenty of time to consider running. I looked for advice from a much-respected man in the community named Harold Cook, the retired plant manager of Hershey's in Stuarts Draft. He's the insightful fellow who advised against the referendum on the fire station issue. When considering my dilemma, he posed two questions. Do you like what you're doing? And do you feel that you are making a contribution to the community?

The first one required some thought. Basically, yes, I enjoyed what I was doing. I liked meeting and working with new people. I didn't like the underhanded motivations and untruths that were thrown out on many occasions. I must say that I liked having a seat at the table and knowing that my opinions and decisions had an impact. I felt that I motivated people to think and maybe see another side to situations or matters. The second question was easy. Yes, I definitely thought that I was making a contribution to our community, very much so.

That made up my mind. I would run for a third term in 2012, along with Tim Williams and Bruce Allen. Williams had someone running against him for the first time since he came on Council. He had also served on the School Board before being elected to Council, and he had run unopposed for that seat, too. Williams represented Ward A, which generally turned out the least voters and candidates, and his opponent was Jim Serba. Serba served in management positions in various nationally known retail stores.

Allen's opponent was Robert Donaldson, a congenial Waynesboro fireman who worked hard at his door-to-door campaign and attended many community functions. He talked with anyone who would listen. Allen didn't see Donaldson as a serious threat, but he campaigned intensely anyway. The newspaper came out against Donaldson, citing that it would be a conflict for a city employee to also be a member of City Council.

Williams, Allen, and I had been in the majority for four years, and sometimes, people want a change just for the sake of change. Those who usually supported our agenda were getting complacent, assuming we would win again. But then, Lori Smith decided to try for a comeback after losing to Mike Harris in Ward D in 2010. Wards A and B were up for re-election, as well as the at-large seat that I held. She didn't live in Ward A or B, so she had to run against me for the at-large seat.

Smith was a formidable candidate who could use the Opportunity Park issue against me. She had lived in Waynesboro all her life and was well-liked. She had served on the School Board as well as City Council. I knew she would give me a run for my money, so I cranked up my ten generals/ten lieutenants grassroots organizing strategy again. I went to work putting up 62 double-sided yard signs, spoke with everyone I could face-to-face, and attended all the community meetings. I made phone calls and sent out a mailer to the citizens who had voted in the 2008 and 2010 City Council elections.

In March of 2012, I ran a letter in the paper declaring my intentions. It reiterated some of what we had accomplished in recent years:

I've worked hard to keep the property taxes low and have voted against every increase proposed during my term. We actually lowered property taxes last year.

In times of economic challenge, we have made the City more efficient....We have not cut services as many would have you believe. We have begun and completed stormwater projects without initiating a stormwater fee, and we've built new sewage treatment and water filtration plants.

We've solidly supported our schools...I have personally worked with the School Board to maintain the strong partnership between it and the Council.

We have invested in economic development. In the March 2012 issue of *Site Selection* magazine, we were ranked as the No. 1 micropolitan area in the state of Virginia and No. 13 overall in the nation for economic development.

(The US Census Bureau defines "micropolitan area" as a rural county whose largest city's population does not exceed 50,000. There are 576 micropolitan areas in the US.)

On the first of April 2012, a month before the election, the local paper devoted its editorial to praise for the 2013 budget. I was quoted as saying, "We've always got

No. 1 micropolitan area in the state of Virginia

work to do, but I think we're ahead of the game."

On April 7, Douglas Norcross, a Waynesboro School Board member, supported my candidacy in a letter to the editor saying:

> My first contact with Frank was shortly after he and a group of citizens, who were concerned about the youth of our city, organized the now flourishing Boys and Girls Club of Waynesboro, Staunton, and Augusta County.
>
> As you can see, he is working for the youth and that means he very much supports K through 12 education. His leadership ability and his skills in managing people are outstanding....

And on April 8, the paper printed letters of support from Lloyd Holloway and Reo Hatfield. So, a lot of positive momentum was in play, and I was feeling pretty good until an episode on April 19 at a forum held for the Council and School Board candidates at the Boys & Girls Club.

A big round of applause for Smith's opening remarks caught my attention. I hadn't realized until that moment that she and two unopposed School Board candidates, Linda Jones and Melinda Ferguson, were criticizing me for failing to act in the best interests of the city's children.

Here I was, sitting in the Waynesboro Boys & Girls Club that I had a large part in establishing, to say the least, being criticized for not acting in the best interests of the children. The candidates were referring to the controversy surrounding the school budget for 2013, and they completely misrepresented my role. They were mostly interested in teacher paychecks, not the children, and did not see the irony in their reproach.

This campaign was hard fought. Councilman Mike Harris was in Smith's corner. And I lost support from my guys at Dave Wolfe's, a low-key political activist group who in the past had worked with me on my campaigns. Wolfe is an admirable guy, and I considered him a friend. He's the one who made the suggestion that solved the school budget problems. But for some reason during the election cycle, he and some of his group decided to back Smith. To this day, I don't know why. I asked him directly on two occasions but never got an answer. Harris and Roger Willets were in Wolfe's group, and I assume they were still sore about not getting the price Willets wanted in the Opportunity Park deal. They seemed to have forgotten that I played a critical role in bringing about the purchase. Or maybe it was because I hadn't supported spending the $8–11 million on infrastructure improvements for the park. Plus, I felt that Harris wanted to be the Mayor, and he probably thought that couldn't happen if I was re-elected.

Smith's public speeches broadly shed light on her Wayne Theatre agenda, which actually fueled my campaign. She was still in favor of the city giving them money, and I knew that the majority of the taxpayers were opposed. I designed all of my ads to reflect her stand and pounced on her whenever she brought it up. I had won in the 2008 election on mostly that one issue, and I felt strongly that I could do it again.

The News Virginian endorsed Smith for the at-large seat. This was baffling because the paper had supported me in 2008, and I had done everything promised. There was a new publisher though, and he had a different outlook on what a City Councilman should be. Evidently Smith was a better fit for that outlook, even though recent Councils deserved some credit for the good work that contributed to the city's stellar ranking in *Site Selection* magazine. When politicians change their outlooks, it's called flip-flopping, but that doesn't seem to apply to newspapers.

During a public forum prior to the endorsement, Smith crowed that the tax rate had come down 15 cents during her previous time on Council. The newspaper printed her statement as fact. But I knew that taxes had only come down eight cents, so I complained to the newspaper and asked for a correction. When questioned about the discrepancy by a reporter, Smith corrected the number and apologized for the error. The most galling thing about the paper's endorsement was that they interpreted her correction as a show of integrity. So, that's the new definition of integrity?!

Then came the biggest blow of the campaign. On the Thursday before the Tuesday election, Mike Harris ran a letter in the Staunton *News Leader* accusing me of back room deals and saying he could not serve with the likes of me, or something to that effect. Here is the letter:

As a member of City Council for two years, I think voters have a right to know how Mayor Frank Lucente conducts city business.

On two occasions, Mayor Lucente promised two different people an appointment to the city Economic Development Authority without consulting council. In each case, after this was known, council appointed other individuals, Jim Hyson and Robert Vailes.

Mr. Lucente and another member of City Council approached the School Board about funding issues without the knowledge of other council members. This effort created unnecessary issues for council in its attempt to address funding issues.

Finally, Mr. Lucente and another member of City Council did make a secret deal to buy the industrial park without the knowledge of three of the council members or members of city staff.

This approach to city business is not what I anticipated when I ran for election, and I think the voters need to make a choice: city business by all council members or city business by Mr. Lucente.

I am very concerned that the voters of this city be informed in order to make the appropriate decisions in this election. As a former member of the military and having had a career with the Virginia State Police, I believe strongly in ethics, and I look for these ethics in our leaders. For these reasons, I cannot support Mr. Lucente for his re-election bid to your City Council.

MIKE HARRIS
Waynesboro

Then *The News Virginian* printed his same letter on Sunday. At least they had enough respect to allow me to respond to the allegations. They ran my response under the headline "Lucente rebuts charges in letter," but the damage was done. As you can see, Harris's letter also implicated another Councilman and slighted the city management, all completely fabricated. I was beside myself. I probably could have garnered a few hundred more votes during that upcoming weekend, but I said, "Screw it—I'm done!" I abandoned my full schedule of campaign opportunities and played golf on Friday and Saturday. I cooked dinner for the grandkids on Sunday and went to a party to celebrate the graduation of a friend's daughter. On Monday, I took it easy and got my poll workers all lined up.

I woke up at 4:45 a.m. on Election Day and got ready to work the polls. At about 7 a.m., I opened *The News Virginian* and found these letters supporting my re-election:

Who is pulling the strings?

I'm generally not a letter writer, but I feel that I must respond to the current character assault on Frank Lucente [Lucente rebuts charges in letter, April 29]. I have known Frank for more than 20 years and have never known him to be anything other than honest and a straight-shooter.

Frank has led this city through a very trying time when many other cities are facing drastic budget deficits and being forced to lay off work force.

One can only hope that Ms. Smith has evolved in her thinking, as she says. But as I recall, in her previous tenure, there is not a tax increase or a spending plan she wasn't in favor of promoting.

I don't know about you, but I have had enough of "change you can believe in."

I shall be voting for Frank.

DOUG WOOD
Waynesboro

Define ethics Mr. Harris

Locals who have followed politics in Waynesboro for many years knew it was going to happen and had predicted it since the last election. Mr. Mike Harris, city councilman for Ward D, finally came out with the "the Smoking Gun" in his recent letter to the editor [Lucente rebuts charges in letter, April 29].

This letter is not about politics or the election; it's about ego and power-seeking. His arrogance and self-aggrandizement finally surfaced as we expected.

Notwithstanding the fact that none of his allegations against Frank Lucente were about violations of law nor anything that he [Harris] has not been guilty of, his words smell of hypocrisy and envy that he wasn't able to get credit for saving the city half a million dollars. If he so much opposed the purchase, or the way it was processed, he should have voted against it. He didn't; he actually introduced the motion to make the purchase.

Actually, most of his allegations could be considered complimentary, including seeking qualified candidates for appointment to boards and commissions.

All current candidates are advocating better communications with the School Board.

To disguise his motives by touting a regard for ethics is ludicrous and laughable at best. Stay tuned and pay attention.

JEFFREY SCOTT SHIFLETT
Waynesboro

Harris irresponsibly touts military veteran status

In response to City Councilman Harris's letter to *The News Virginian*, published April 29 ["Lucente rebuts charges to letter"]:

Honor and ethics are inherent fundamentals of every military member, especially of us retired veterans. So, when I see someone like Councilman Harris touting his veteran status and implied honorable and ethical standards, I expect some standards to be upheld.

Mr. Harris says he believes strongly in ethics and that he looks for ethics in leaders. Ethics require a strong leader to take action when something occurs. Ethical and honorable behavior are not waiting until just days before an election to throw a fellow Council member under the bus in a blatant attempt to influence an election. If Mr. Harris truly believed what he wrote, then why did he not take action at the time of the incidents he alleges?

As a member of the Waynesboro City Council, Mr. Harris has a duty to protect and serve the people of Waynesboro. So, Mr. Harris, by his own admission, has either failed the people of Waynesboro or is using his position to discredit a fellow Councilman for his own political ambition.

It appears that Mr. Harris is using a façade of armor and ethics to further his political ambitions while discrediting Mr. Lucente. Obviously, Mr. Harris has no concept of the true meaning of honor and ethics.

STEVEN J. LAURENZO
Waynesboro

These lifted my spirits immensely. I was surprised and heartened that people had come to my defense spontaneously. Usually a politician has to solicit letters of this nature. Confidence returned, and I spent Election Day at the polls alongside lots of volunteers who pitched in to help me. I was surprised that Nancy Dowdy supported me this go round and had even invited me to put a sign in her yard. I don't really know how this shift of allegiance came about, but I was certainly pleased to have her support. She even came to my celebration! Greg Bruno of waynesboro.com found it noteworthy and posted pictures of her with Williams, Allen, and me on his site. Politics really does make for strange bedfellows, but I had genuinely liked Dowdy as a person ever since I met her back in 2002.

I waited for the results of this tumultuous election. Here are some notes from my journal on Election Day:

> At 6:52, I left the polls and went to the Boys & Girls club. Many people were already on site. I brought in the food and the sodas and settled in for the count. First precinct in was A, and I won 177 to 97, up 80 votes. I lost Ward B by 14 votes and I won Ward D by 17. The calmness left me as I knew it was a race....The next word I got was that we had swept [the race], meaning all three of us had won: Bruce, Tim, and myself. I was relieved. I won by 137 votes. I lost B by 14 votes and won the other wards: D+17, A+80 and C+49....I was disappointed that I didn't beat her badly, but I won.

I held my at-large seat with 52 percent of the vote. Allen held Ward B with 57 percent, and Williams barely held on to Ward A with 50.4 percent of the vote. Four years ago, I had won in a landslide. Now, here I was winning by just 137 votes.

When I got home, my wife asked if I was happy with the outcome. I told her how disheartened I was with the numbers, that I thought I should have won by a much greater margin. I retired to my bedroom and tried to sleep.

At about seven the next morning, I was awakened by a call from Tom Sheets, a friend who owned Blue Ridge Lumber. He wanted to congratulate me on my win and the margin of victory. I said, "Hell Tom, I only won by 137 votes!"

(L-R) Me with Bruce Allen, Nancy Dowdy, and Tim Williams at our victory party

Photo credit: www.waynesboro.com

He said that considering what I was up against, it was a landslide victory. The letter from Harris, the newspaper endorsing Smith, the special interest groups, Wayne Theatre, teachers, government employees, the Dave Wolfe group, etc. And then it dawned on me that he was right. I'd had a lot working against me to say nothing of the self-inflicted damage of the last few days when I gave up and went golfing. My attitude turned around just like that. I was a reinvigorated man grateful for the opportunity to serve Waynesboro for another four-year term. That morning's headline in *The News Virginian* read "Lucente Remains." Sounded like it had something to do with death to me. From my journal that day:

This was a day of congratulating. Everybody called to tell me how much they had done for me. One guy said he had made 200 calls for me on Monday and Tuesday.

But I knew the people who had really done the work, and I thanked them. Yesterday, the newspaper printed three stinging letters in response to Mike Harris's letter. I think they helped me, and I wanted to acknowledge that. I made sure my signs were coming down… and I paid Nancy Wells for her help with the campaign.

Wells had spent many hours researching voters, addressing envelopes, and doing all the administrative work needed to run a campaign.

Tim Williams had won by only 23 votes in his first contested race. Tonya Hardy who had done so much to clean up the Commerce Street apartments, called her 40 tenants and encouraged them to vote. I am afraid if she had not done that Williams would have lost. Wells and Hardy are perfect examples of how just one committed citizen can make a big difference in so many ways. I can't say this enough: Get involved!

The election was over, but there was some unfinished business. The staff and other Councilmen wanted to do something about Harris's letter. He had questioned my integrity and honesty as well as that of another Councilman who wasn't named, and he offended the staff by ignoring the essential nature of their role. I was already over it, vindicated by winning the election, but the staff and other Council members were looking for a way to exact retribution for his insults.

The staff took it upon themselves to ask Harris for a public apology, one that they and four Councilmen would approve. He was warned in writing that failure to comply would result in Council putting a letter of censure in the public record, expressing formal disapproval for what he had printed in the two newspapers prior to the election.

Harris brought in his lawyer, Roger Willets, one of the men who sold Opportunity Park to the city. Willets' counter was milk toast,

There was some unfinished business.

and no agreement could be reached. So, a special Council meeting was called for Friday, May 11, 2012. Staff read the following statement:

> We the undersigned Waynesboro City Council members would like to express our concern over a letter written by City Councilman Mike Harris and published in the local newspapers just prior to the election.
>
> To be clear, Mr. Harris had every right to publicly endorse a candidate of his choice. Likewise, he has the right to criticize the record of an incumbent member of Council. We believe, however, that some of the content of Mr. Harris's letter could undermine the confidence that the public has in the City Council as a body and the statements could mislead the public as to how the City Council

and the municipal organization conduct business. We would address the allegations listed in Mr. Harris's letter as follows:

As to the allegations that the Mayor promised appointments to the Economic Development Authority: Every individual who serves on a Waynesboro board or commission does so based on their merit and willingness to serve. Potential candidates for boards and commissions may be recruited by members of City Council, current or past members of those boards or commissions, or their fellow citizens. Candidates often come forward on their own initiative. Mayor Lucente has certainly encouraged individuals and the public generally to serve on local boards and commissions. Every candidate for a board or commission must forward a letter of interest to the Clerk of Council, and the Council as a body evaluates and selects members to City boards and commissions. No Councilman could unilaterally assure an appointment.

As to the allegation that the Mayor and another member of Council, without the knowledge of Council, approached the School Board regarding school funding issues:

Mayor Lucente and other members of Council periodically discuss school funding issues with individual School Board members. On occasion, these discussions result in proposals and suggestions to the school or City administrations or to the respective elected bodies. Most often such conversations are simply intended to maintain healthy dialogue. The City Council can only act by majority vote on matters of funding, and it is inaccurate to claim that Mayor Lucente made a unilateral proposal to the School Board.

As to the allegation that Mayor Lucente and another member of Council made a "secret deal" to buy the industrial park without the knowledge of the other three members of Council or the City staff: The Council is concerned as to how this statement could be misconstrued. The City Council's decision to purchase industrial property at Exit 96 was actively deliberated by the City Council for more than 18 months, even predating Mr. Harris's election to City Council. During that period of time, the Council directed the City staff to conduct numerous investigations of the property and its potential for industrial development. The City staff met frequently with individual members of Council and met with both the City Council and the Economic Development Authority in closed sessions, as is permitted under Virginia law. To be sure, the issue was hotly debated, and Mayor Lucente and another member of Council made an issue of purchase price both privately and during the various meetings with the Council. At one point, the Mayor and another member of Council threatened not to support borrowing money for the purchase unless the price was lowered.

The deal to purchase the land, however, is very much a matter of public record. The contract to purchase was made public, distributed to the press, and was made available on the city website. The city staff and the Chairman of the Economic Development Authority presented the proposal to the City Council in a public meeting. The decision to purchase was delayed to allow for additional public review. The decision to purchase was approved by the unanimous vote of City Council in a public meeting.

To claim that there was any deal other than the one reflected in the public record is false and unfairly undermines the integrity of the City Council and the administrative staff of the city. To this we take strong exception as we do not accept Mr. Harris's claims as an accurate portrayal of our actions in regard to the purchase of industrial property at Exit 96.

Council voted 4–0, with Harris abstaining, to record the letter in the minutes of the meeting. Now, we could begin our new term.

In the course of all the unpleasant controversy surrounding the campaign and election, a very different sort of letter had landed in my mail just before Election Day. This one made me smile:

Dear Mr. Lucente,

A few days ago, we received your campaign letter and card.

We were both pleased to note that while a computer printed out address labels for each of us separately, they were placed on the same envelope. That saved you 45¢ postage, plus the cost of one each of card, letter, and envelope. We think that is a good example of efficiency in government.

In addition, many of the political appeals for funds we have been receiving are sent to one of us, usually the husband. This leads to a perception that a wife does not count, even though she is a registered voter. So, both of us appreciate the recognition on your part, and/ or the staff you have helping you in preparing these mailings, that this wife does count. We thank you.

Incidentally, the monthly reports we get from our Medicare supplement pharmacy invariably arrive on the same day in separate envelopes. That company, we suspect, is spending too much on postage. We recognize they might say it is more expensive to try to mail them together in one envelop—in terms of time involved to assemble the mailing. We don't know that.

Thank you for the example in stretching your campaign finances.

Whether you win re-election or not, we wanted to let you know that we appreciated your stewardship of resources and recognition that a wife counts, too.

Sincerely yours,

Thomas E. Shoemaker and Anna G. Shoemaker

I met with Harris and told him I had put the matter of his letter behind me. We were going to be on the same Council for at least two more years, and I vowed to work with him for the betterment of the city.

In the two months after the election, I had my golden retriever taken away for 16 days because he was deemed dangerous, had a kidney stone removed by emergency surgery, and got behind in my work. On July 2, 2013, my term as mayor ended, and I had done my best. I took a lot of heat for two years, and I had been an open target. I had learned that I am more effective working in the back than in the front.

CHAPTER 16

My Dangerous Dog

Early in the evening on Memorial Day 2012, I was working in my garage with the door between the house and the garage slightly ajar. The garage door leading out to the street was also open letting in a warm breeze. My golden retriever, Luke, came out to the garage to visit with me. He's usually content to stay close unless he's enticed by a squirrel or a dog.

Before I knew what was happening, Luke bolted out the garage door after Mr. Layman, who was walking his dog the way he did every day. Luke is usually limited to barking at them through a front room window, but today, he saw his chance and took it. All I could do was shout, "He won't bite!"

Luke sounded ferocious, but he was seven years old and had never bitten a person or animal in his life. Layman lifted his little seven pound dog up over his shoulder and turned away in case of an attack. Showing behavior he had never shown before, Luke bit Layman on the leg. I caught up and seized control of my dog immediately. He rolled over on his back exposing his belly in a submissive position.

I asked Layman if he was okay, and he said he was. He rolled up his shorts, and we saw a couple of punctures. I apologized and suggested he go get the bite checked out, offering to pay any medical bills. He agreed to see the doctor because he had diabetes and couldn't risk an infection.

Then Luke and I went back to the house, and Layman went on his way. After thinking about it for a few minutes, I decided to look in on him. His house was only about two blocks away. He was still out walking his dog, but I caught up with him. Knowing Layman to be a dog lover, I took a chance and offered to put Luke down. To my relief, he said no. I again suggested he get the bite looked at and offered to pay the medical bills. I said I would check back later after he had seen a doctor, and then, I returned home.

I thought that was the end of the matter, and I vowed to never let Luke get outside off-leash again. The next day, Layman said everything was fine except for a little soreness. But he called me back several hours later with news that the Animal

Control Officer (ACO) had contacted him and requested an interview. He said he wasn't really interested in talking with the officer; he preferred to just forget about it. I was all for that, and hung up thinking everything was okay.

But it wasn't okay! Two days later, my wife called me from home and said that a police officer and Dee Price, the ACO for the city were taking my dog away for 10 days of quarantine. I rushed home to find out that under the relatively new dangerous dog law, a dog that bites a person has to be quarantined for 10 days in case of rabies. This law applied even though Luke was current on his rabies shots. The law gives the ACO the discretion to let the owner keep the dog quarantined. But she chose to take Luke to the pound because she had let some others keep their dog at home, and the dog had strangely disappeared. Now her policy, as well as that of the police chief, was to impound all dogs, no exceptions.

I was devastated. Luke had never even been boarded and now he was going to the pound. He was part of our family. When my wife and I traveled, we hired a sitter to stay home with him.

I could go to court and fight or accept him being classified as dangerous. Classified as dangerous meant that he had to be neutered, an identification chip would be implanted, dangerous dog signs would be posted around our house, he would always be on a leash as well as muzzled when off property, if outside on my property, he had to be inside a fence built to specifications, we were forbidden to use the city dog park (which I had helped establish), and there were requirements for insurance in case of future bites. There was no question about it, we were going to court!

I visited Luke at the pound where he was caged alongside numerous wildly barking dogs. The second day, I noticed his tail was bleeding, so I asked to move him at my expense to my vet's boarding facility, Woodworth Animal Hospital. My request was granted. There he had a building to himself, and I walked him every day.

It's sad and painful to be separated from a beloved dog, particularly at night. The truth of the matter is that it didn't bother Luke half as much as it bothered me. He seemed to adapt to the routine very quickly. Dogs live in the present and go with the flow. On the third day, I was walking him on a leash around the hospital grounds when suddenly he was attacked by a pit bull that raced from a nearby house. I was screaming, "He is killing my dog!" as I tried to pull the 80-pound pit off of Luke. I was hysterical. Luke was trying to get away, and the pit bull kept lunging at him.

I finally got the leash off of Luke and put it around the pit bull's neck and dragged him away from Luke. The owner was just standing there watching in shock. I asked her to hold the leash while we got out of there. I looked back, and the pit bull was pulling her along still following us, but we made our escape. Her dog was big and strong, but he looked to be around 11 years. If he had been in his prime, it would have been a different story.

It took a while for me to calm down once we got back to the safety of the animal hospital. The employees took Luke back to assess his injuries, and I noticed I had been bitten on the hand. They reported some superficial cuts and bruising on Luke. He was okay, but I had to go to the hospital to

We were going to court!

have my hand checked out. My wound was cleaned, and I was discharged.

Any dog bite generates a report to the Health Department and that in turn is sent to the Police Department and then on to the ACO. That's how they had been alerted to Luke biting Layman. A day or so later, the ACO called me to get an interview about the pit bull incident. I told her the story as it happened. She responded that Luke's quarantine had to be extended for seven more days as she couldn't discern whether the pit bull or Luke had bitten me. Anytime someone gets between two dogs and gets a bite, both dogs are quarantined. I told her that the pit bull bit me, and it wasn't Luke's fault. He was trying to get away. She wouldn't take my word for it. It was seven more days of isolation for Luke. He did his time without further incident. When he came home, it was as if he had never been gone, but I was definitely not over it.

On June 15, 2012, Luke's dangerous dog hearing was held in general district court in Waynesboro. Judge Helvin was substituting for Judge Heatwole, who recused himself because he knew me personally. Judge Helvin was from Charlottesville, the district adjacent to Waynesboro. He didn't know that I was the Mayor.

Every step of this ordeal was reported in *The News Virginian* and on Television 29 News. Luke's trial brought out several of my political adversaries. A fellow named Jackson called the prosecutor's office to report that he had been walking by my house when Luke charged him barking. No bite though. Several other people called in to say that Luke had barked at them. One person reported that my dog had chased and rolled her dog at the leash-free park. These people were more than willing to testify against us at Luke's trial, and they did.

There were reporters and TV cameras in the courthouse, and the Judge looked befuddled but allowed them. The evidence was presented, and the Judge declared Luke to be a dangerous dog. I was very disappointed to say the least. The trial right after ours was to determine whether the pit bull that bit me was dangerous. I was a witness, and that dog was also found dangerous.

After the trial, my attorney told me that the court had planned to dismiss the charges against the pit bull, but how could they charge my dog and dismiss the other one? So the pit bull met the same fate. We immediately went to the Clerk's office to file an appeal to the circuit court.

Painter, the owner of the pit bull, was there to file an appeal also. He said that he was told not to worry, that he didn't need an attorney, as they were going to dismiss the charges against his dog. He was very upset when the tide turned.

My attorney warned me not to expect much on appeal. If the Judge rules the dog not dangerous, and the dog bites another person later, it puts the Judge in an awkward position. For that reason, I was putting my faith in the American Jury Trial system. I'm a strong believer in jury trials.

I felt certain that this was not a case against my dog but a case against me. I was going to spend a lot of money on a defense attorney for Luke! Now my years in local politics were coming back to bite me.

Early in the spring of 2012, several months before this incident, the police department had requested that City Council hire a second ACO. My comment at the time was that there wasn't enough work for the one we had, and there was no need to hire a second one. The current ACO had not taken kindly to my comment.

And in 2005, after I first took office, I had noticed that the prosecutor's office was not in the city building. Instead, he was practicing in an office he owned, which the city rented from him and paid to keep clean. I asked the City Manager if we had room for him in the Gorsuch Municipal Building. Yes, we did. I suggested it would save some money to move the prosecutor into the city building, and that's what happened. I had campaigned for the prosecutor when he first ran for office, but he was not happy with me after that.

He could have plea bargained this case down to something less, but he was determined to try it. I did a little research and found out that Waynesboro averaged at most two circuit court trials a year. Our city has the usual crimes of other cities our size:

robbery, embezzlements, child porn, assault and battery, murder, etc. Most all of these cases are plea bargained, but no, my dog and I were going to trial because this was a very important case to keep the streets safe for our children.

Preparation for trial began. I asked my attorney, John Hill, if he wanted to handle the appeal, but I warned him it could damage his reputation. Who would put their fate in the hands of an attorney who couldn't get a golden retriever off the dangerous dog registry? I wanted to approach the trial from the angle that this trial was vindictive and had nothing to do with Luke, but Hill wanted to try it on the merits of the case.

It seemed the law was on our side. The Virginia Code says, "No dog that has bitten, attacked, or inflicted injury on a person shall be found to be a dangerous dog if the court determines, based on the totality of the evidence before it, that the dog is not dangerous or a threat to the community."

Luke barks a lot, but as soon as you enter the house, he'll start licking you and begging you to pet him. He's full of personality, and those who know him think highly of him. He's great around children. We had strong witnesses, and this was a single incident, so I wasn't afraid to go with the merits of the case.

The trial was held on May 9, 2013, at 9:00 a.m. It lasted all day, and then the jury went out for deliberation. A question came to the judge: If it was found that Luke was not a dangerous dog could the ACO still have some control over the dog? The judge responded that it was the jury's job to decide whether or not Luke was dangerous, but not their job to have any say in the consequences of their decision. After a total of 90 minutes deliberating, the jury of seven came back with the verdict: Luke was indeed a dangerous dog.

So much for the jury system. Never the less, that was the verdict, and I would abide by it. As I left the court building, the press asked if I would appeal again. No, the jury had spoken, Luke was a dangerous dog, and I would abide by the law. The appeal for the pit bull was never acted on, and the case was dropped. There were only two other dogs designated dangerous in the city at that time. They are German Shepherds, both belonging to the same owner.

This was a great learning experience for me. I got to be the defendant in a trial. When it didn't go my way, I had to change a few practices in regard to my dog, but he was oblivious to all of this, and my pain was more heartache than hardship. Attorney fees came to $10,000 dollars. I pay around $500 a year for insurance on Luke. He's 12 years old as of this writing and still in good health. He and I take walks in the county now, as he is not allowed at the leash-free park. He likes the county better anyhow because he has the place to himself.

Luke and me arriving for our routine of walking children to school about six months prior to the dangerous dog episode

CHAPTER 17

The Trash Issue

In the spring of 2015, while looking forward to a relaxing day on the beach in Duck, North Carolina, I noticed a garbage truck picking up trash along the street. What caught my attention was that the driver had no helpers on board. He operated an automated arm from inside the truck. It lifted up a trash can and dumped the contents into a hopper on the front of the trash truck. He repeated the process over and over again as he moved down the street. Once the front hopper was full, he operated another control inside the truck to lift the hopper up and over the top of the truck and deposit its contents into a larger container in the back of the truck. The name printed on the door of the vehicle was Waste Management. I always got a little excited when I saw potential to save Waynesboro's taxpayers some money, and this process looked promising.

I called the city of Duck that day and inquired about their trash service. They told me that they had a contract with Waste Management, and they paid for it with money obtained from property taxes. I was intrigued by the prospect and planned to do some research as soon as I got back home.

Waynesboro manages its own waste removal business servicing a little over 7,000 residential customers. Small private waste haulers were contracted by hundreds of additional customers at that time. Generally speaking, only large companies can afford the huge capital outlays required to do the job city-wide. I learned that Waste Management is one of the nation's leading providers of curbside waste removal services.

Any resident can sign up for the city's service by simply calling into City Hall and making the request. The monthly fee was $14.50 as of my research in 2015. This covered a weekly pick up, and the city provided one 96-gallon trash can per household. The service also includes two annual bulk trash pickups using the knuckle boom truck.

The city did not offer curbside recycle service, but we did have a recycle center that received recyclable waste that residents brought in. You separated it yourself and deposited it into different containers designated for glass, cans, aluminum, plastic, newspaper, cardboard, and office-type paper. The amount of recycled material that the city collected in this manner satisfied the federal and state recycling requirements for a city of our size, but just barely.

I stored my recyclable items in my garage and took them to the recycle center once every two or three weeks. But it was a chore, and keeping trash in your garage is not desirable. I had done this for 13 years because I hated to see reusable things go to the landfill, and I believe recycling is good for the planet.

I knew that the city's waste removal business was being subsidized by tax dollars and local industries because the fees being charged to the residents weren't high enough to cover the actual cost. Even though the garbage department had become mostly self-supporting back during my first term, we occasionally had to take money from the general fund for trash related expenses.

At one time, Waynesboro had its own landfill but now all of the waste collected is transported to Jolly View, a regional landfill operated by the Augusta County Service Authority. It is owned by the three local governments: Waynesboro, Staunton, and Augusta County. When private haulers and commercial and industrial entities transport waste to the landfill, they pay a $45 per ton tipping fee. But

Waynesboro city's trash business does not pay the tipping fee that the other haulers pay.

Instead, when it comes time to close a cell (unit) of the landfill, or open a new cell, the city has to pay its share of the cost from its general fund. Millions of dollars had been taken out of the general fund previously to close the retired landfill owned by Waynesboro. And we still bear the cost of monitoring the methane gas that is generated from the waste that is now buried underground. We also have to continually drill wells and test the water to make sure the buried waste is not contaminating the water table. These monitoring procedures are expensive and ongoing for 30 years.

When the Jolly View cell that's currently in use reaches capacity around 2020–21, it will close, and the city will have to pony up more money to pay its share of the cost for closing it and opening a new cell.

Each municipality's share of the landfill costs is based on its percent of the total usage. For example, if the city of Waynesboro, its residents and businesses, etc. generated 25 percent of the refuse dumped at the landfill, Waynesboro would be responsible for 25 percent of the total costs of operations including closing and opening of cells. Anyone required to pay the landfill tipping fee is screened to determine whether they are from the county or one of the two cities. The tipping fees collected from those users are credited to the accounts of their respective localities. Jolly View is a great example of governments working together to provide solutions in a manner that spreads the burden and lowers the cost for the taxpayers. The shared arrangement eliminates the need for duplicate expenses, services, and procedures.

I began looking into the matter of private haulers. I called the County Administrator for Augusta County and found out that the county did not provide trash service. He told me that he had worked in another county once where none of the trash workers showed up one day because they were all out with injured backs. I recalled that we had a lot of turnover in our trash department, and we were subject to liability for our workers' injuries.

Being exempt from tipping fees gave the city an unfair advantage over private companies. I learned that if Waynesboro had to pay the tipping fees it would cost the city approximately $326,000 a year. If that $326,000 per year could be collected from a private hauler such as Waste Management, $30,000 of it would cover our operation fee at Jolly View, and $296,000 would be left in the city's account to pay its share of future landfill cell closures and openings.

There might even be some money left over to cover some of the expenses related to Waynesboro's retired landfill.

The city would save money, and we would be out of the trash business. The city also had a Refuse Fund that held about $796,000 in reserve for the trash business. This money was used to buy equipment such as trucks and trash cans. I found out by talking to Waste Management that if they got the contract to take over the trash business, they would buy our inventory of trucks and such for approximately $1.2 million. That would free up the $796,000 held in the Refuse Fund for other needs. That adds up to $1.996 million dollars that would be available to the city quickly, and there'd be $296,000 a year in our landfill account from now on.

Being out of the trash business would ease up work on the city because complaints from our citizens about trash pick-up were our most frequent complaints. I found other benefits as well. Private companies could offer curbside recycle service. I took an informal survey of many residents and found that they would recycle if we had curbside pick-up, but would not as long as they had to sort it and store it and take it to the recycle center. If we had curbside pick-up there would be a big increase in the recycled material collected in our city.

We've talked before about the private sector being more efficient than the government when it comes to most things. This is demonstrated by just one man working the trash truck at the beach. The city has a crew of three men on the trash truck. One man drives and two ride on the back of the truck, jump off, pick up the can and place it on the lift that dumps it into the back hopper, house by house. One man works one side of the street and the other man works the other side of the street. When the truck is full, the two

We would be out of the trash business

men jump into the cab with the driver, and they all ride to the landfill to make the dump. Round trip to the landfill probably takes at least an hour with three men on the payroll.

I felt that the information I attained through my research supported the idea of going with a private hauler because of all the benefits mentioned above. I began looking for the downside, and the one thing I discovered was that 16 city employees would lose their jobs. Rob Clendenin of Waste Management told me that an employee who operates one of their trucks is better paid than employees in the city's trash removal department. He said he would give our laid-off employees priority when hiring for the Waynesboro routes if the city went with his company. He obviously would not need to hire all of them, but the ones who were hired would be better paid. We could give the others buyouts, or give them first choice on other jobs that became available with the city in the street department, water department, or sewage department, etc.

I had spent a couple of months learning about privatizing trash removal, and it was time to make my presentation to the staff and Council. I have a deep respect for the staff of our city. City Manager Mike Hamp and Assistant City Manager Jim Shaw are both outstanding public servants, highly educated with the utmost integrity and honesty. They have a lot of influence over Council because they are the authorities on how the city operates.

That's not to take anything away from Council members, but by design they are not involved in the daily operation of the city. Council appreciated the management team of Hamp and Shaw because they knew their roles and did not attempt to make policy. They sometimes swayed Council by sharing pertinent information as well as their opinions, but they followed the Council's decisions.

I knew if I could get the staff on board with the privatization concept, I would have a chance to get this through the Council and make it happen. I first informed Council of my discovery. I asked them to keep an open mind saying I would get back to them shortly with details and pros and cons. Then I went to the staff to make my pitch.

I explained all the benefits and the only disadvantage I could think of. They listened intently, but their reaction was negative from the get-go, and they expressed the need to check my research and numbers. The city's trash business was well run. It broke even and was even backed for depreciation by that reserve Refuse Fund of $796,000. I could see that the thought of garbage collection no longer being in their domain was a problem.

They wanted to assemble some Refuse Fund data and offer an opinion on the financial impact of eliminating the fund by privatizing. Hamp put together a comprehensive report including a spread sheet. The long and short of his response was in this statement: "The analysis indicates this plan would not be in the best interest of the city."

I talked with Clendenin, and he agreed to come to Hamp's office and make a presentation to Hamp and Shaw and Mayor Allen in July. He fielded a lot of questions and responded to the staff's doubts. By the end of the meeting, Hamp and Shaw said they would continue looking into the possibilities. I got the sense that it was a lost cause.

I began sharing details with Council members. Williams said he would support changing to a private hauler, but I couldn't get a real read on what the others were thinking. It felt to me as if the staff had already lobbied the Councilmen. Some might have believed the city could manage garbage more efficiently than the private sector, but I thought I had presented plenty of information to the contrary.

My friend Mayor Allen and I were sitting around his kitchen table when he made the comment that he didn't want the city to lose control over the garbage business. That was the same argument the staff had presented early on. At that moment, I felt my influence and ability to impact change slipping away and knew then that I would not run for reelection in 2016. But I persevered. I wanted the public to have a say.

Hamp kept dragging his feet when it came to putting a privatization presentation on the agenda for a regular Council meeting. After months of procrastination, it was finally scheduled for the December 14, 2015, meeting.

But on the Friday prior, I was called into the City Manager's office to be told about a last minute agenda item. The staff wanted to present a resolution in support of giving $1 million to the Virginia

Museum of Natural History in hopes of locating it in Waynesboro. The grant would be a combination of financial aid, in-kind support, and real property.

I balked because I knew that would grab all the attention and be the story in the newspaper the next day. The privatization of trash collection would be lost. I explained my opposition to the staff and the Mayor, but the staff persisted in saying we had to do this right away or the state would think that we didn't support the museum being built here. I reminded them that the state legislature didn't meet until January. What was the rush? I told them that if they insisted on doing this, I would vote against it. I knew they wanted a unanimous vote for PR reasons, so they backed off and moved the resolution to the December 28 meeting. (The museum was never located in Waynesboro because of the lack of state funding.)

Clendenin participated in the meeting on the December 14 making a power point presentation that emphasized the curbside recycling benefit. He pointed out other Virginia municipalities that his company serves including Charlottesville, Blacksburg, Luray, and Williamsburg. Statements made by Hamp were recorded in the minutes:

Staff's position was that privatizing the refuse collection service would not improve service or improve the financial position or stability of the Refuse Fund. Analysis showed that savings would be marginal, short-lived, and eroded by even minor adjustments to the assumptions outlined. The Refuse Fund is well operated and provides good service and has financial stability.

The City Manager reviewed the common motivators to privatize including the inability for the locality to financially sustain operations or replace or maintain capital equipment and external market factors that negatively impact service delivery. He asked Council to keep in mind that the information provided at the December 14 meeting was not a proposal but rather a concept. If Council proceeds with privatization, the Code of Virginia requires undertaking a formal proposal process.

Council was provided with current facts including the number of residential and commercial customers, staffing, annual collections since 2011, and that the last rate increase occurred in 2008. Also reviewed were the list of services currently provided by the Refuse Fund, the Fund's financial status and performance, and other Virginia localities' experiences with privatization of refuse collection, noting that unlike many localities, the City of Waynesboro does not require residents to subscribe to City refuse service. Hamp concluded by noting Waynesboro's ownership and operation of refuse collection provides accountability and facilitates responsiveness, it demonstrates financial stability, provides favorable customer service, and allows for open market competition and citizen choice.

After all was said and done, Councilmen Williams and Marks and I were in favor of having a work session to discuss the matter further. The Mayor was absent during the meeting, but Council agreed that when the Mayor returned we would schedule a session.

If the people would support this there was still a chance, but my hopes were slight because as I've said time and time again, it's very difficult to get the people involved. That same day *The News Virginian* ran an article on the subject. Hamp is quoted as saying, "I think we're exploring solutions to a problem that staff doesn't agree exists."

When I spoke with citizens and gave them details, they were all highly supportive. But no one stepped forward to call other Council members or write a letter to the editor, and no one came to any meetings to voice their support. A work session was finally held on March 3, 2016, but my proposal to privatize garbage collection went nowhere. If I could not get this no-brainer passed I could not get anything done.

Years ago, Ted Barr, an old-timer who was the elected sheriff of Cabell County, West Virginia, shared some words of wisdom while encouraging me to stick with politics. He compared a tomato to a politician. He said that at first the tomato is green like a politician just learning the ropes. Then the tomato turns juicy and red and everybody wants a slice. This is the stage where the politician is in his prime and does what he came to do. Then in a grave tone, he warned that the tomato eventually rots and no one has an interest in it any more. It's a corny metaphor, but that's where I was in my political career—the rotten tomato.

I had realized back in September that my inability to gain support for this project meant my time was up. I announced then that I would not seek reelection. My hope was that someone truly qualified to help the city would step up, and I wanted him or her to have plenty of time to campaign.

CHAPTER 18

Stormwater

Some people say we can colonize Mars or the moon. These are two very inhospitable places to live temperature-wise, and there's no air to breath, food to eat, or water to drink. It's not happening. We have to take care of the planet we have. Waynesboro's well-designed stormwater management system is a fundamental step in that direction.

Stormwater issues were already under consideration when I was appointed to Council in 2005. The city had identified and categorized 28 projects that needed attention. The top eight addressed the potential for extreme flooding, causing health issues and damage to properties. Homes were affected during heavy rains due to backed up drainage infrastructure and malfunctioning stormwater ponds, etc. But previous Councils had not made long-term system-wide solutions to the stormwater issues a priority.

It wasn't just a local concern. Waynesboro is located within the Chesapeake Bay Watershed. Fast moving stormwater carried our motor oils, sewage, garbage, weed killers, and other toxic household and industrial chemicals directly or indirectly into our streams, which ultimately found their way to the Bay, destroying wildlife all along the way. I strongly supported the implementation of a comprehensive stormwater management program. It was just a matter of how to make that happen.

In order to pay for solutions, the City Manager wanted to create a stormwater utility. From 2006 to 2008, it went back and forth between Council and staff and consultants, but we were unable to agree on even a basic a plan. Initially, I objected to taking on new projects before we had a program in place to maintain the infrastructure that we already had. For instance, at that time, we had over 100 stormwater retention ponds throughout the city that had been built to meet requirements before various new construction permits had been issued. There were no requirements for upkeep though, so they were left unattended and eventually lost their ability to retain stormwater. Either the drains were clogged causing the ponds to overflow, or the wall surrounding a pond had collapsed or washed away. I remember one small pond was turned into a flower garden because the building owner had no idea it was intended to be a stormwater retention pond.

We had a Public Hearing on the subject in late 2006, and as usual, the general population did not attend. One purpose of the meeting was to discuss a stormwater utility fee structure.

In a natural environment, stormwater percolates down into the ground, which acts as a filter for pollutants. But cities are covered with man-made impervious surfaces such as roofs and parking lots that repel and divert stormwater so that no natural filtering can occur. Impervious surfaces caused the problems when it came to stormwater run-off, so it made sense that a fee should be based on the amount of impervious surface each land owner had on his or her property.

We decided the fee would be established in units. A unit would measure 1,500 square feet. A property of less than 1,500 square feet would still be considered one unit. The fee per unit would be $3 per month. For example, if your home's roof is 1,500 square feet or less, it would have been considered one fee unit; 1,500–3,000 square feet would have been considered two fee units, and so on. If you were a business or industry, then we would have counted your roof and all of your paved parking lot. Invista's fee with its roofs and parking lots totaling 4,000 units, would have added up to $144,000 per year.

When the businesses realized that this would cost them some serious money, they suddenly wanted in on the discussion. Even the Chamber of Commerce got involved. Initially, I was in favor of creating a Stormwater Utility supported by a fee structure of this sort. As I mentioned earlier, I worked closely with the City Manager to separate water, sewer, and garbage fees from the general fund. And I continued to like the idea of managing utility fees exclusively for the intent of the utility.

But as time went on, I began to pay attention to Councilman Williams and Mayor Reynolds who did not want to put another fee in place. They wanted the money to come out of the general fund, arguing that the citizens were already paying for stormwater management by paying their property taxes. In a sense, I could not dispute that.

Reynolds thought that we should pay for the stormwater management through the general fund, but that would mean raising taxes. Williams thought we could pay for it out of the general fund without raising taxes. I had always felt that our government could operate more efficiently, so I sided with Williams, believing we could provide improved stormwater management without raising taxes.

Smith and Dowdy were in favor of instituting the new utility and charging the proposed fee. Smith accused me of jumping ship when I changed my position. I have often observed that once an office holder stakes out a position, he or she is very reluctant to let it go. It seems to be about winning. But I have always done considerable research and kept an open mind. I responded to Smith that I was trying to do what I felt put the least burden on the citizens. We have to be open to changing direction if and when new insight comes into play.

> **I could see no reason to raise taxes.**

I reasoned that the fee being considered would put an unnecessary burden on the businesses, some of which were barely hanging on as it was. Reynolds asked us if we would vote in favor of a tax increase, and Williams said he would, but only if he had no choice. I said I would go along with the program being funded through the general fund, but I could see no reason to raise taxes. With that, Reynolds stated that funding would come from the general fund, and that was the end of the staff's effort to establish a separate stormwater utility.

For the next eight years, the stormwater projects were funded by the general fund, plus a few loans that were re-paid with general fund moneys. We completed several of the top priority projects during that time and made great progress in the area of stormwater control. We didn't have to raise taxes to accomplish these things because economic growth increased the city's revenue. Jumping ship, as Smith accused, had saved the tax payers a lot of money.

But then at the regular Council meeting on January 27, 2014, we were informed that Waynesboro had been designated by the Department of Environmental Quality (DEQ) as a small municipal separate storm sewer system called an MS4. The designation required that the city obtain a national pollutant discharge elimination system (NPDES) permit, and develop and implement a program to minimize the discharge of pollutants passing through the city's stormwater system to waters of the state. We had to comply or be fined by the DEQ and the Environmental Protection Agency (EPA).

I raised questions about the agencies' authority and whether or not Congress was going to give us the money to cover this new expense. An EPA representative cited specific sections of the Clean

Water Act, which mandated the establishment of the MS4 program, and no, there was no federal money available for this program.

The early cost estimate to develop and fund the program was a little less than a million dollars a year and could grow to as much as $1.6 million a year. On May 27, 2014, at a regular Council meeting, we passed a Stormwater Ordinance amending the City Code to integrate the city's new stormwater management requirements with the existing erosion and sediment control requirements creating a unified stormwater program. This followed a Public Hearing on the matter where once again, no one from the general public spoke.

For about a year, the Council and the Stormwater & Flood Advisory Commission, organized to give input to businesses and residents who would be affected by the fees, went back and forth on how to fund the stormwater program. Council finally settled on funding the program entirely with a stormwater fee rather than the general fund.

If we used general fund money, we would have to generate an additional 42 percent to give to the schools in keeping with our commitment to contribute 42 percent of discretionary spending to their budget annually. So, if we spent $580,000 on the program, we would have to generate $420,000 more in revenue to cover the schools. That made no sense. By establishing a fee structure exclusively for the stormwater program, we avoided giving the school any portion of the moneys collected. In essence, we had formed a new utility that worked like the garbage, water, and sewer departments, rather like what we had discussed years earlier.

This new stormwater utility was modeled on the state stormwater management program. The elements of the new program included 160 ponds, 55 miles of storm sewer, seven miles of ditches, 2,534 inlet structures, and 557 outfalls. Some of this had already been completed over the last eight years, one piece at a time.

The state program also includes public education, pollution detection and elimination, infrastructure maintenance, and control of construction site run off. It requires good housekeeping for municipal operations, encompassing all public works including street sweeping, recycling of oils and other chemicals used by the city, leaf removal, and recycling.

On May 11, 2015, we had a Public Hearing on the establishment of a stormwater utility fee. A complex fee structure was proposed and unanimously passed by Council at the next regularly-scheduled Council meeting on May 26, 2015. The residential fee is based on a 1,600-square foot measurement called the Equivalent Residential Unit (ERU), and the cost per ERU ranges from $1.72 per month to $6.84 per month depending on the size and type of the residence. Non-residential is figured using a different formula with a cap of 244 ERUs. Some credit is given to business properties that include stormwater management facilities on-site so that their waste water never reaches the city's system. The largest non-residential property in Waynesboro is Invista at 400,000 square feet and they pay the maximum of $10,000 per year.

Establishing the formula took long hours of research by the staff, the Stormwater & Flood Advisory Commission, Council, and consultants. I believe that we came up with a reasonable system that is fair to both residents and industries. This was an essential process for the health and vitality of our community and the protection of our planet, and I was proud to play a part in making it happen.

CHAPTER 19

The Budget Process

Budget time is a time when everyone talks over everyone else, seeing only their own point of view and accomplishing little. It reminds me of those tabloid talk shows on television, which seems to be the new pattern of interaction for our society. Budget time is one of the few times that people will show up to participate in Council proceedings.

In May 2012, we held a Public Hearing to establish the 2013 budget. Twenty-five citizens signed up to speak. The first one opposed the Council allocating more money for the schools. I wondered if he regretted speaking up after the next 17 spoke in favor of more money for the schools. One of the non-profits made a plea for Council to continue funding their organization. Three people requested additional funds for the tourism department. A motel owner wanted the city to fund better lighting for the areas around motels

and restaurants. One representative of the Police
Benevolent Association requested more money
for the police department. Someone took the
opportunity to complain about the separation of
church and school, and another thanked God for
schools and teachers.

Every bit of the city's money comes from
taxation. The majority of Waynesboro's residents
don't want their taxes raised, but there is a stigma
associated with stating that in a public meeting.
I suppose they fear they'll appear to be cheap or
needy. Paying taxes is a hardship for many, but as
I mentioned before, there are others who might see
a benefit in higher taxes, and they will argue that
taxes should be raised. I chose to keep an eye on
the big picture in order to hold the city's spending
down and save the taxpayers money.

Every February and March, the City Manager and
office staff formulate the upcoming year's budget.
The new fiscal year starts July 1. Council is generally
not involved or informed during the budget making
process. It takes months of meetings with various
department heads and the Finance Director to
develop the all-inclusive document. Even with the
previous year's budget as a guide, it was still an
enormous task that occupies the majority of the City
Manager's time.

By Virginia Code, the staff must present the budget to Council by the first Monday in April of each year. At the end of the presentation, Council receives a copy of the proposed budget for the first time. Comprised of around 125 pages of numbers, the document can be daunting. Most people who serve on Council do not have a financial background and therefore lack the experience and skill to really evaluate these budgets. I have a little experience reading financial reports and budgets due to my profession. By no means am I an expert in the field of finance, but I have always been pretty good with numbers and have some common sense when it comes to the relationship between money and getting a job done.

When I was first elected to Council, I advocated that the City Manager consult with Council members during the budget making process. I thought it would be useful for staff to have advance input on matters such as whether we would support a tax increase, raises for City employees, adding employees, and new programs, etc. This would avoid clashes in the public Council meetings. But the two City Managers that I served with both preferred to present their budgets in a public setting, making a case for acceptance of each line item as they went along.

Once the budget has been presented, there's time for work sessions to study and discuss the proposed budget during April and May. Council operates with an add/delete list to record the items they wish to change. For example, if the City Manager has requested a new employee for a department and Council does not approve, that item and its associated costs would be entered into the delete column. In addition to keeping the taxes low, my goal has always been to find ways to make cost-effective improvements. I have spent countless hours hovering over the budgets, looking at every detail of where the money comes from and where the money goes.

During my first term, Doug Walker was the City Manager and numerous budget work sessions were scheduled for Council each year. But they were mostly dog and pony shows with department heads making lengthy presentations about the role they played in the city government. They talked about how much money they needed and what they needed it for. I didn't find the presentations particularly useful in making budget decisions.

As time went on, there was turnover on Council as well as staff and these work sessions morphed into simple discussions and the department presentations were abandoned. Gradually there were fewer and fewer discussions and Council members became more and more inclined to just go with the City Manager's recommendations.

Along with the budget presentation, the City Manager suggests a real estate tax rate proportional to his proposed budget. If Council agrees with the tax rate, the budget is not affected. But if Council feels the proposed tax rate is too high, the budget has to be recalculated to reflect a lower tax rate. The city raises about $173,000 for each penny on the dollar that is added to the real estate tax rate.

During my 11 years on Council, the tax rate was raised once and lowered once. So basically, the rate remained flat, yet the budget increased from $31,412,173 in 2006 to $46,951,410 in 2017. That's a 49.5 percent increase in 11 years attributable to

They were mostly dog and pony shows

growth in the business sector: Walmart, the Town Center, the movie theater, new restaurants, and the construction industry.

The staff has to figure out how to work with the quirks of each different Council. For example, in the spring of 2013, Council was of a conservative nature, so the staff knew it would be difficult to get a tax increase passed. They can count on some of their funding requests being denied, so they always ask for more than they need.

With that mindset, the City Manager went for a three-cent property tax increase to off-set his 5.2 percent increase in the budget. His recommended budget for 2014 was $43,699,564, which was $2.1 million over the previous year. He built a strong case for the tax increase, but Council saw it as non-essential and turned him down. The city ran smoothly without it, saving the citizens $500,000 that year.

For 2015, he asked for a two-cent property tax increase on the $44,800,000 budget. That's a 3.5 percent increase adding up to $1.5 million over the 2014 budget. Council did not approve the increase.

For 2016, he asked for $45,700,000 which was a 3.3 percent increase over the 2015 budget. This included a one-cent property tax increase. Council did not approve the increase.

On March 23, 2016, the City Manager presented his budget for the 2017 fiscal year that would begin July 1. The budget increased by $1.3 million or 2.86 percent. He did not ask for a tax increase because now the city had an additional million dollars annually in revenue thanks to the Town Center being paid off. And there was an annual savings of

$750,000 in the general fund as a result of the new stormwater fee.

Council was given a chance to review the budget prior to the first work session scheduled for April 13 at nine in the morning. As usual, I spent hours poring over it, and I had some questions.

The meeting started on time, but one Councilman was late, and Williams was not there at all. Mayor Allen asked me to start with my questions, but I didn't want to start while two Councilmen were absent. They would be voting on the issues, and I wanted them to understand my positions. I reluctantly went ahead, and after about 15 minutes, Councilman Freeman arrived, and I had to start all over again.

There were a number of issues I was hoping to address. For starters, the City Manager had been asking for an additional person in the Human Resources (HR) Department for many years. Council had rejected the request every year. Another person on the payroll adds about $50–60,000 per year permanently. I had researched some large private and non-profit businesses to learn how many people worked in their HR departments per total number of employees. The ratio was one HR employee per 200 employees. Our city had a little more than 300 employees and two people working in the HR Department. I felt we were fine.

On the other hand, we had been getting complaints from the citizens about the snow removal program. Most of the localities around us had a pretreatment program. When snow was in the forecast, they pretreated the roads with a chemical solution that cut down on moderate snow and ice build-up, helping to keep roads clear and safe. This would mean a one-time investment in equipment that cost about $50,000, and our street department could provide the man power. So, my suggestion was to buy the equipment, reasoning that this would be more beneficial to the community than an additional person working in the HR Department.

One of my colleagues commented that if the City Manager didn't need an HR person, he wouldn't be asking for one. Another felt that the street department was doing a good job of snow removal and didn't feel we needed to do the road treatment. No one brought thoughts or questions of their own to the session, mostly just comments contrary to my suggestions.

Raises for the employees had been put into effect in January, the latter half of the 2016 fiscal year. That amount would double once the raises were budgeted for a full year. I wanted to know how we planned to pay for the raises once the 2017 fiscal year began in July. The staff didn't answer my question and the rest of Council didn't seem to be concerned. I also asked where the $750,000 that had been used for stormwater would go now that there was a stormwater fee being put into effect. The staff said some was going to schools as a one-time contribution over and above the usual 42 percent of our budget. They offered no information

Council did not seem to care.

about the use of the rest of the money, and again the other Council members seemed indifferent. There wasn't going to be a tax increase and evidently that was all they needed to hear.

I was discouraged. The energy I put into trying to improve upon the disposition of the taxpayers' money was a waste. Based on the way this session had gone, I said I did not see the point in any more discussions. The council seemed happy with the budget as presented. And I found out later that Williams, who was also ending his term, had relayed to the Mayor that he was good with the budget as it stood.

I had brought some legitimate concerns to light, but Council did not seem to care. I gave up and accepted the budget as it was. On May 23, the budget was approved by Council basically as presented on a 4–1 vote. I was the one against.

I have already explained that failing in my attempt to move the trash business to a private hauler convinced me that I was no longer effective on Council. My inability to influence the budget process for the sake of the taxpayers was more of the same. No longer effective possibly in part because I was now a lame duck. My term would end on June 30, just a few months away.

The following year with Council seats filled by Vice Mayor Terry Short, Elzena Anderson, Jeff Freeman, Mayor Bruce Allen, and Alvin "Pete" Marks, taxes were raised seven cents, approximately a 10 percent increase. The city's 320 employees whose salaries make up around 80 percent of the budget once payroll and benefit packages are rolled in, were given an additional raise of one percent effective July 1, 2017, six months after the previous raise. The one percent raise cost the city another $149,554.11 per year. And salaries only go up, they never go down.

By far the City Council's most important job is to set the tax rate and approve the annual budget. The taxes the citizens pay and the services they receive from the local government are critical quality-of-life factors determined by the annual budget. The approved document gives the city the authority to receive and spend all the moneys for the upcoming year. If a spending measure is in the budget that has been passed by Council, the staff has the authority to spend for that measure without any further discussion. The City Manager calls it his budget, but once Council members approve it, it's Council's budget and they have to answer to the public.

Most people have no idea that the city's employees got two pay increases that January and July of 2018, the same year in which there was a 10 percent increase in property taxes. This is what happens when the citizens become complacent and fail to pay attention to what's going on in their government. Unless people who exhibit true leadership ability step up and run for office, I fear that this city will soon become overburdened with expenses and debt to pass on to future generations.

CHAPTER 20

Working Together

I've made a point of emphasizing that as a general rule, our citizens don't get involved in the city's decision-making processes and projects, and that is certainly the case when it comes to the government functions. But that's not the case when it comes to special projects or community events such as the Fall Foliage Festival, Soap Box Derby, Apple Days, and our Fly Fishing Festival. These events are mostly planned and carried out by what's called the citizen sector, groups of creative and energetic volunteers. They provide entertainment for locals and their visiting friends and families and foster a sense of community pride. I'm particularly proud of the annual Chili Blues & Brews Festival.

I went to Colorado about twelve years ago and happened on an event in Silver Creek called Chili Days. We relished the live music and food tents and drank a beer or two. Our friends sampled the whiskey from the whiskey booth and were allowed to keep the glasses as souvenirs. It was a pleasurable time, and I was inspired to bring the concept back to Waynesboro.

I presented the idea to Council as a plan to increase tourism. With the exception of being a nice place to fish, Waynesboro had no scenic appeal, and in those days, there were not any real tourist attractions. I thought we could draw people to Waynesboro with an event like Silver Creek's Chili Days.

The Council gave me the green light, and then I presented the idea to Waynesboro Downtown Development for their consideration. One of their members stepped up to help organize and run the first Chili Blues & Brews Festival, which has taken place every September since 2007.

In many regards, entertainment, recreation, and lifestyle features are just as important as essential services when it comes to attracting and maintaining a vital population. The greatest lifestyle advances in Waynesboro's recent history are scenery and environment restoration projects, both spearheaded by the citizen sector.

In the late 90s, a group of community-minded volunteers formed the 20/20 Committee to consider some new projects that might make the city a more interesting place for residents to work and play. They put out a survey to get some feedback about several possible projects. The idea of developing a greenway was the most popular. A greenway is a walkway through undeveloped land near an urban area, set aside for recreational use or environmental protection. Some residents had seen greenways when traveling through other communities and were enthusiastic about having one in Waynesboro.

Since it was the most popular idea, the City Manager asked for someone on the committee to head up the project. Jim Nichols said he would do it with the stipulation that he would get to put together his own committee to develop the project. Their first step was to ask the Director of Parks and Recreation to bush hog a path along the South River on the south side of town in Ridgeview Park. Removal of overgrown trees and underbrush opened a pathway through the woods, exposing Virginia bluebells and other wild flowers for walkers to enjoy. This first effort was met with such enthusiasm that the committee pushed the city to move the project forward.

The City Manager instructed staff to apply for some federal grants to pay for an engineering firm to plan and design the greenway's path through the city. The staff's attention to the project was sporadic, but slowly some progress was made.

When I came on Council in the spring of 2005, the greenway concept was described to me, and I thought it was a very worthwhile project. There had been delay after delay in starting the first phase, a mile-long stretch between Wayne Avenue by the YMCA and Main Street along the South River. The hold-up was in getting the necessary easements across two private properties, the old Crompton Company land and DuPont land, which was no longer in use.

Waynesboro greenway

The Crompton holdings were owned by Beverley Shoemaker who lived out of the area. She was very enthusiastic about the greenway, which complemented an expensive remediation brownfield project that was underway to upgrade her land and buildings. She was quite cooperative in removing some drainpipe that crossed the greenway site and emptied into the river. DuPont was overly bureaucratic about the easement request and took their time in answering correspondence. But the easements were finally granted and now it came down to finding money to do the project.

Jim Nichols had talked with me about his vision for the greenway. We met at the river and walked from Main Street north through the woods along the river to North Park, and he told me he didn't think he would live to see any part of the project completed. I decided then and there to do what I could to get the first phase completed during his lifetime.

We had federal grants that the Virginia Highway Department was to administer, but they dragged out the process month after month by failing to communicate. The ball was dropped in City Hall for long periods because of changes in personnel and a new City Manager coming on board in 2008. But Jim Shaw, the Assistant City Manager, took it upon himself to move the greenway to a front burner and things began to happen. There were numerous hurdles caused in part by property owners who actively protested having the greenway near their homes. If people would tune in to other aspects of government the way they do in NIMBY situations, the world would be a better place.

On March 13, 2012, the first phase of the greenway was finally dedicated and opened to the public. Because of Nichols's long dedication to the greenway going back into the late 90s, I forfeited my spot as Mayor to speak at the dedication and offered the honor to him. He graciously accepted.

Once the residents saw first-hand how the greenway enhanced our community socially and aesthetically, enthusiasm and support for its extension and completeness increased. On June 3, 2017, we dedicated phase two, and the city is actively working on phase three.

While doing some research for this chapter, I asked Jim Shaw how phase three is progressing. It will run through the woods along South River all the way to North Park and will be the most peaceful and scenic section of the greenway. He responded that the project was at a standstill because the McCutcheon family refused to grant the city an easement across their property. Some of the staff had tried to convince them but had not succeeded.

I asked if he would mind me giving it a try. He gave me the go ahead saying that if I could get the easement, it would be a great legacy for me. I wasn't looking for a legacy and didn't know exactly how I would proceed, but I wanted to make it happen for the community. The solution came up in a casual conversation with my editor who lives in Lexington. She had seen a similar situation there when the city was having difficulty gaining an easement in order to complete a new neighborhood street. It was resolved by naming the street after the homeowner who allowed the essential easement.

This was a great idea! I went back to Shaw and asked if that part of the greenway could be named for the McCutcheon family. He didn't see why not, so off I went to talk with Jean and Carl. I had been acquainted with them for years and had served on some boards with Jean. After much discussion, they took the offer under advisement and said they would talk it over with their kids. A week or so later, they contacted me, and we met again. Carl said they did not want the greenway named after them, but they had decided to sign off on the easement because it would help to bring the community together. And now, the kids can safely ride their bikes from one end of town to the other without crossing a single street.

I told them how the idea of naming the greenway came about. Jean asked if I would give her a signed copy of my book when it is published. I assured her that I would, and that's the only copy I plan to give away. If nothing else, my small contribution to the solution for completing the greenway has made writing this book worthwhile.

A highly-prized natural feature of Waynesboro is the South River that runs right through the middle of town. Approximately six miles upstream of Waynesboro, feeding the South River, is the single largest complex of springs of any place in Virginia. The total volume of water from the four major springs located less than a quarter mile apart is approximately 12,000 to 14,000 gallons per minute. According to Urbie Nash, a retired local Environmental Engineer who lives in Waynesboro and has researched the South River extensively, there is no other place in Virginia that has spring fed flows of this magnitude entering a stream in that short a distance. In low flow conditions in the summer, more than 90 percent of all the water in South River entering Waynesboro is from this uncommon spring complex.

This should make for ideal living conditions for brown and rainbow trout because they flourish in the cool waters provided by the springs. But Nash, who lives on the river and is an avid fisherman, noticed that the trout stocked by the Department of Inland Game and Fisheries each year were not really thriving in the Waynesboro stretch of South River. He recruited some experts at Trout Unlimited and began tracking the temperature of the water. They discovered that the water in proximity of the Rife-Loth dam was unnaturally warmer than the water upstream.

The 10-foot high, 200-foot long bridge was five feet thick and had been built in 1907 to replace an older one which was built in the 1880s by Waynesboro resident Alexander Rife. Rife needed increased horsepower to run his Ram Works foundry. The original dam was lost in a flood, and the Rife-Loth Dam, or Ram Works Dam as it is also called, was rebuilt with limestone in 1907. You might remember the Rife name as one of the founders of the original Wayne Theater.

Over time it had become a liability.

At first, the dam was an economic asset for the city, but over time it had become a liability. Accidents at the site of similar dams were being reported around the region, and the dam was in bad repair and was degrading the river's eco-system. It blocked fish and eels from traveling upstream, and it kept kayakers and other paddlers from navigating the river. It compromised the health of the trout population, which kept Waynesboro from becoming a significant tourist attraction as a year-round trout fishery.

It was obvious to Nash and others that the dam had to go. It was owned by the Ram Works Homeowners Association (HOA), which consisted of 70 townhouses along the riverbank above the dam. It formed a little lake right in their backyards that was enjoyed by those residents as well as homeowners who lived upstream closer to the Ridgeview Park. Many people had bought homes in the area specifically because of the beauty and recreational environment that the dam facilitated.

You can see what Nash was up against. He began talks with the HOA to see if they would give the go ahead to remove the dam. Chester Campbell, president of the HOA, told Nash that the dam would come down "over his dead body." He had a long history working for Ram Works in an office right next to the dam, and he'd lived beside it for many years. He was quoted in the local paper as saying he'd raise the windows and let the water rolling over the dam lull him to sleep at night.

Nash was at a dead end. It was at this time that I became aware of his mission and joined in the campaign to restore the river to its natural free-flowing state and temperature. He told me of the potential for the river, and I asked him for the names of the 70 members of the HOA. Consideration of the private dam was not a function of Council, but in my mind, this change would be good for the entire city.

I began calling on the homeowners and explaining the benefits of dam removal. I convinced some, but others had objections including presumed loss of property values, creation of unsightly muddy banks as the river water receded, etc. Some of them thought the whole exercise was orchestrated by a bunch of elitists who wanted the dam removed to enhance their own fishing experiences. I really enjoyed the lively discussions and made some new friends. We had the better part of a majority willing to go along with the removal, but the decision would be made by the five-member Board of Directors of the HOA. They were all firmly against it, especially Campbell.

A year or so had passed when Nash received a call from Campbell. He wanted to talk about the dam. It seems that the depth of the river near the dam was eroding a retaining wall, and it could cause great problems to the residents if it failed. And it was getting harder and harder to get liability insurance for the dam due to recent drownings in other cities and law suits filed against the dam owners. Nash suggested that if the dam was removed, some of the building material and debris could be used to shore up the retaining wall. And of course, lowering the water level would help reduce the erosion. Plus, the need to insure the dam against liabilities would disappear. Nash said he thought he could get the dam removed at no cost to the HOA.

Nash and Campbell began working together in earnest to bring about the removal of the dam. The HOA was on board, but opposition continued to come from those who lived further upstream. They came up with all sorts of arguments and petitions, but they didn't offer to help pay for essential repairs to the dam or the retaining wall. It was estimated that the repairs would cost three times what removing the dam would cost.

The Waynesboro DuPont plant, now Invista, has been situated a quarter mile downstream from the dam for more than 90 years. The plant used mercury as a catalyst in fiber production between 1929 and 1950. During that time, today's strict handling and disposal regulations did not exist, and the mercury waste was discharged along the banks and into South River. This serious contamination problem was discovered in the 1970s extending all the way downstream into the Shenandoah River. In spite of continual remediation efforts, the mercury level in South River remains high to this day. DuPont offered Nash the money for the Rife-Loth Dam removal, a gesture to assuage some of the community's negative feelings toward their past treatment of the river.

With funding in place, the Ram Works HOA signed an agreement in 2011 to remove the dam. The South River now flows free again for the first time in more than a century. Within days of the demolition, paddlers were said to be crossing the former dam's boundary and members of the Shenandoah Valley

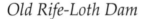

Old Rife-Loth Dam

Chapter of Trout Unlimited were seeding the newly exposed riverbanks.

The water temperature has lowered by six degrees. The trout are more than thriving now with reports of 16-inch brown trout being caught. There is a far more robust population in the river year-round. Eating the stocked trout is not allowed. The sport is strictly catch-and-release because, Nash says, the large trout are quite expensive to stock. The mercury does not pose a health problem for the stocked fish because they are not raised in the contaminated river. He is amazed to see some small wild rainbow trout these days, meaning that some reproduction is beginning to occur. The mercury could render the wild fish unsafe for human consumption, time will tell.

South River now provides Waynesboro with wildlife diversity and beauty and has become a very popular destination for trout fishermen who come from all over and spend their money in Waynesboro's hotels and restaurants. I was very glad to play a small role, but we have Urbie Nash to thank for this extraordinary achievement. He worked tirelessly for years to restore the river to its natural state and still works to make the river and our environment healthier for future generations. He says that the effects of removing the dam have exceeded his wildest expectations.

CHAPTER 21

Moving On

The 2014 election was really not an election at all. It was more of a self-appointment day. Mike Harris who had written the letter against me, the staff, and an unnamed Councilman in 2012 never redeemed himself. He knew he couldn't beat a challenger. He dropped out of the running when attorney Pete Marks announced he would run for Harris's Ward D seat. Jeff Freeman ran unopposed for his Ward C seat. It's the only time I can remember when there was no competition.

The day after the election, *The News Virginian* lead story began with this excerpt:

"Low turnout for city elections"
Waynesboro saw one of the lowest voter turnouts in its history Tuesday, with just 2.9 percent of the registered voters casting a ballot.

All total, there are 12,256 voters in the city, and 356 went to the polls Tuesday.

"This is very low," said Lisa Wooten, Waynesboro's general registrar. We had 22 percent two years ago. This is very low."

In June of last year, the primary only had 150 people cast a ballot....

There was no competition for the School Board races either. And here's part of the editorial that ran in *The News Virginian*:

"Little ballot choice? Then run for office"

Less than 20 minutes. That's how long it took many of us to vote yesterday as Waynesboro elected new representatives from Wards C and D for the City Council and School Board....less than 10 percent of the registered voters came out to cast a ballot.

Throughout the day, we heard several reasons for that. Some people told us that they just didn't care because it wasn't their ward's representative. Others complained about candidates but said they didn't have time to bother. There were also those who complained about the lack of choices, thinking that there was no need to vote because the winners had already been decided. By far that was the argument we heard the most throughout the day—residents wanted choices, they wanted multiple people to pick from.

To change that, people have to be willing to run for elected office, which is harder than one might think. It takes about 15 or 20 minutes of our day to cast a vote. After that it's our responsibility, as informed citizens, to keep up to date about issues.

One of the things we heard during the day was that there's no information released about any of the candidates. When we pointed out that each one was covered in individual stories [as well as] the one on the April 23 candidates forum—and then our website and social media updates—the people admitted that they hadn't actually read any of those, which is their option.

For an elected official, there are weeks, months, and years of work put into not just the campaign but what comes after.

At last week's Waynesboro budget session, Council members had to juggle family events and work schedules to find the time where they could all meet for another discussion on the budget.

It's not as simple as showing up for two meetings a month, and that's it—or one if you're a School Board member.

And therein lies the problem. It's hard to find people willing to give up that much time in their life for a four-year period to serve the city, and those who do should be applauded.

We would like to thank each of them for being willing to give their time and serve their fellow citizens.

To those upset over the lack of choices [who] didn't vote as a result, we encourage each of you to consider putting their names in the running when the next seats come open.

All three of the City Council seats that were up for re-election in 2016 were contested races, and two of three School Board races were also contested. But still only 19 percent of Waynesboro's registered voters bothered to vote.

This book exemplifies and emphasizes the worrisome trend that our citizens are failing to participate in the governing processes. Fewer people run for office, fewer people vote, and apparently fewer people care what's going on outside their personal world. No matter what the reason, this failure will lead to the loss of our democracy, our freedom, and our quality of life.

My days on City Council are over. I've had the utmost respect for all of my Council colleagues. Serving your community as an elected official is demanding and sometimes thankless work. It was always my goal to serve Waynesboro well. I was recently telling my family that a friend of a neighbor had referred to me as "the one who ran the city into the ground for the last ten years." My daughter commented that the woman was probably aggravated because I hadn't voted to raise taxes and spend more money [on her pet projects]. I am definitely guilty of that!

Our citizens are failing to participate.

One of my greatest sources of pride is the fact that we were able to accomplish all that's mentioned in this book and more while sustaining a level property tax rate for eleven years. We undertook much-needed capital projects that directly or indirectly affected the health and well-being of Waynesboro's residents, yet we increased the city's reserve funds from about $4 million to $13 million in that timeframe. When I left Council in 2016, the city was in excellent financial condition.

I put some energy into candidate selection for the City Council election again this year (2018). The political process gives a sense of purpose to my old age, and I intend to stay with it as long as I am able. I can't fathom not doing my part for my community and country.

"Lucente will not seek city council reelection"
    November 19, 2015, Staunton *News Leader*
    WAYNESBORO—After 11 years serving on the Waynesboro City Council, Frank Lucente will not seek a fourth term in 2016.

Lucente was elected to the board in [2005] and has served as both mayor and vice mayor during his time on City Council.

He said he feels that he has given to the community, and it's time for "new blood" to take over.

"It's a tough job," Lucente said, "And I'm getting up there in age. It's time for these young people to step up and be more involved."

That's why he is announcing early his intention to not run again for city council—he wants to give the citizens of Waynesboro as much time as possible to decide to run for his seat, which is the at-large position.

Lucente said he is proud of many accomplishments during his time on city council, especially those that encouraged a more "fiscally

It's time for "new blood."

responsible" city, such as growing the city's reserve fund from [$3 million] in 2003 to $13 million now.

"We're not in deep debt...we have the reserves," Lucente said. "And downtown is vibrant."

Interview with Harrisonburg TV station WHSV 3

WAYNESBORO, Va. (WHSV) –

Timothy Williams and Frank Lucente have served Waynesboro for 23 years combined.

"Eleven years went by pretty quickly," said Lucente.

"The last 12 years has been a great experience," Williams said.

Williams was elected in 2004, while Lucente was appointed to City Council a year later in 2005.

Both men have done much for the city while in office. Williams and Lucente both are happy not having to raise taxes for the people. It's the increased budget that [makes] Williams proud.

"The fact that we've grown our revenue by $20 million in 12 years," said Williams. "That's over a $1.5 million a year on average."

Despite the success, Lucente said there will still be issues to tackle.

"The elementary schools—we have to work with them. The stormwater thing, these regulations, federal regulations are getting stronger and stronger, and it's costing the tax payers more and more money," said Lucente.

As the two men finish out their last month in office, they said they're ready for the next chapter.

"Just ready to retire, retire and enjoy my grand baby and just enjoy civilian life for a while," said Williams.

"It was a very, very good experience for me," Lucente said. "I've always wanted to write a book, but I never had anything to write about. Now I do."

Both City Councilmen will serve until June 30. The two new members who replace them are Terry Short, Jr., and Elzena Anderson.

"Retired Councilman departs with complex legacy"

By Bob Stuart [from *The News Virginian*] / Posted: Saturday, July 2, 2016 8:11 p.m.

WAYNESBORO—The legacy of just-retired Waynesboro City Councilman Frank Lucente is a complex one.

To his friends and those who served with him, Lucente is a fiscal conservative who has kept taxes low, worked to increase the city's financial reserves, and incurred no more debt than was necessary.

To his critics, Lucente has taken his spend-thrift ways to myopic extremes by opposing adequate funding of core city services such as education, they say, and by failing to articulate a sound vision for the city's future.

After nearly 300 Waynesboro City Council meetings and more than 11 years as a member of that body, including a stint as mayor, Lucente retired from local government last week.

The 71-year-old successful businessman and CEO of two companies, Lucente plans to write a book about his local government experience.

"I want people to understand how government works and how we get to where we are," he explained. He said he hopes to both inform and entertain readers with his book.

Lucente took office in the spring of 2005, after the Council appointed him to fill the unexpired term of Chuck Ricketts, who left to become a district judge. He subsequently was elected twice to full four-year terms, including the last time in 2012.

He was the driving force behind the creation of the Boys & Girls Club of Waynesboro, Staunton, and Augusta County two decades ago. He is proudest of such milestones as the opening of the Waynesboro Town Center development, the increased employment at PGI, Inc., a renovated Kate Collins Middle School, and the development of the city's Coyner Springs water plant.

He has also held a tight rein on spending—too tight some would say, especially when it comes to the number one issue on many residents' minds: how to replace the aging Waynesboro High School. Lucente, however, steadfastly believes the city can't afford to spend the more than $70 million needed for a

He hopes to both inform and entertain.

new high school and thinks renovation is the likely route for the facility.

He has also held firm on his opposition to contributing funds to the Wayne Theatre. It's a special interest of the arts that the majority of the people (Waynesboro residents) would never attend, he said of the theater. "I didn't think it was a project city taxpayers should fund."

Clair Myers, who served as Executive Director of the Wayne for more than 10 years until recently transitioning to emeritus status, takes issue with Lucent's description of the Wayne. He said Lucente "has had a very limited understanding of what the re-opened Wayne Theatre would mean for the city."

Myers said Lucente should have taken a look at the programming the local theater has provided since opening in March, and "the range of admission prices from 'pay what you will' for films to children's shows at, or less than, other area venues.

"Or the Broadway quality shows at prices for lower than at [similar] theaters," he said.

If Lucente had looked at all that and the other benefits the Wayne Theatre brings to the community, Myers said, "He would have had to reconsider these pronouncements."

Myers said Lucente also has not checked on the economic impact the theater has on local restaurants.

But other local leaders say that Lucente has been generous in helping those in need.

Waynesboro Family YMCA Executive Director Jeff Fife worked on the founding board of the Boys & Girls Club with Lucente. He says Lucente "has been relentless in finding resources for kids in our community, especially kids from our impoverished backgrounds."

Other controversies will no doubt be a part of Lucente's legacy.

He sued *The News Virginian* in 2006 for defamation, claiming the newspaper had damaged his reputation with an editorial regarding a city election. Circuit Judge Humes Franklin Jr. dismissed the suit, saying the piece was not defamatory.

In 2012, Lucente's golden retriever, Luke, bit a pedestrian walking by his home and was cited by the city. Lucente fought the case, which ultimately went to Waynesboro Circuit Court. In 2013, the dog was judged dangerous by a jury after an hour deliberation. Lucente estimates he spent $10,000 in legal fees on the case, and still must keep his dog in a fenced area and muzzle the dog when it goes out for walks.

And while he strongly supported the city's $3.475 million purchase of the Exit 96 [Opportunity Park] industrial park, he has continually opposed spending to provide the infrastructure for the property. He calls the land purchase a good investment, and one that "would provide something for the economic development director to sell." But he thinks spending millions on water, sewer, and other infrastructure is not wise unless there is development.

About the Author

Frank S. Lucente was born in Detroit, Michigan, in 1945. His family moved to Fairmont, West Virginia, when he was two. He grew up and went to school there through college graduation. After serving in the military for three years, he moved to Huntington, West Virginia, to attend graduate school. Lucente married his wife, Betty, there in 1972. They raised three children in Huntington and moved to Waynesboro, Virginia, in 1990.

CPSIA information can be obtained
at www.ICGtesting.com
Printed in the USA
FFHW02n0003031018

9 780999 288566